A Time to Knit

Ann Kingstone

A Time To Knit

In loving memory of Kenneth Gordon Leach

Published by Ann Kingstone Designs
www.annkingstone.com

ISBN 978-0-9569405-3-7

Contents

Spring

A time to knit…
4–5

April (short sleeved jumper)
6–10

Dilly Dally (socks)
11–15

Truly (shawl)
16–21

Summer

A time to knit…
22–23

Glade (lace cardigan)
24–30

Prom (full length gloves)
31–35

Summer Seas (stole)
36–39

Autumn

A time to knit…
40–41

Indian Summer (wrap)
42–46

Mallorn (jumper)
47–53

Sweetheart Mitts (fingerless mittens)
54–57

Abbreviations and Symbols
75–76

Winter

A time to knit…
58–59

Adore (heart decoration)
60–2

Anwen (coat)
63–71

Avé (slippers)
72–74

Thanks
77

In the spring I have counted one hundred and thirty-six different kinds of weather inside of four and twenty hours. ~Mark Twain

Which nicely sums up the problem facing us when we wake on a spring morning; what to wear?

Luckily, there are fibres that have thermal qualities which keep us both warm in cool weather and cool in warm weather. My favourite of these is wool. A light wool jumper or cardigan is a necessity in spring.

Also, spring is the time when I get wander-lust. With strong urges to go off walking on our beautiful English hills, a pair of warm wool socks is an essential spring knit too.

Finally, a medium weight shawl is ideal for spring as it is so easy to throw on or off to suit the very changeable temperatures.

April

Dilly Dally

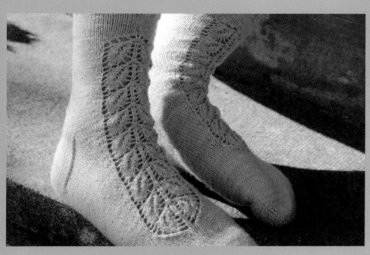

Truly

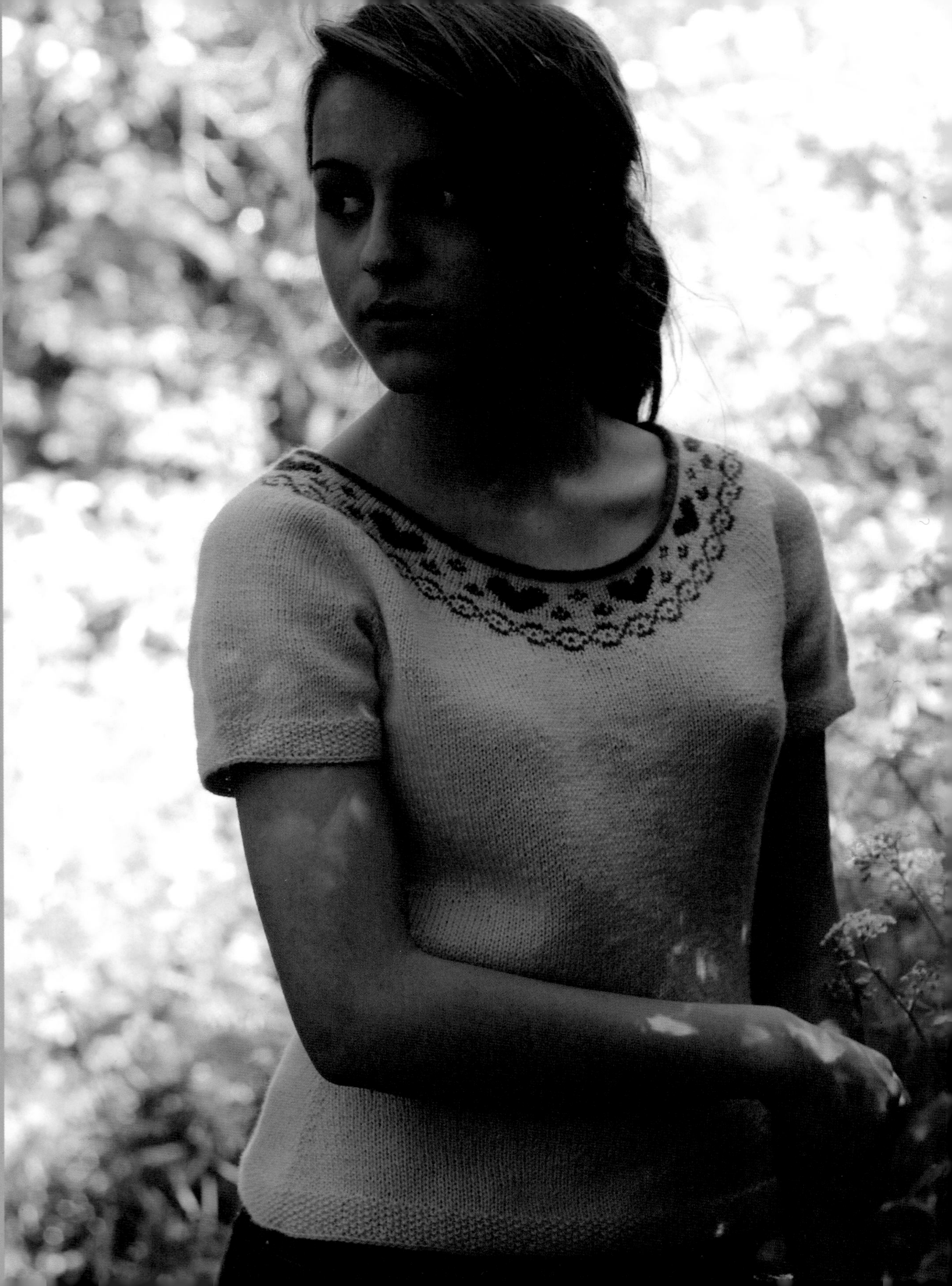

SIZE

To fit 32(34:36:38:40:42:44:46:48:50:52:54:56:58)" chest with 0–1" of positive ease.

MATERIALS

4ply/fingering weight wool yarn with approximately 165 metres /180 yards per 50g. You will need a 50g ball/skein in each of 4 contrasting shades for the yoke, and 4(4:5:5:5:5:6:6:6:7:7:7:7:8) 50g balls/skeins of your chosen main colour.

The pictured sample was knitted with Susan Crawford 'Excelana' in 'Cornflower Blue' (A), 'Powdered Egg' (B), 'Ruby Red' (C), 'Alabaster' (D) and 'Nile Green' (MC).

NEEDLES AND NOTIONS

2.75mm/US 2 and 3mm/US 2½ needles for your preferred methods of small and large diameter circular knitting

Adjust needle size as necessary to achieve the specified tensions.

Four stitchmarkers. 3 small safety pins.

TENSION/GAUGE

26 sts and 36 rows per 10cm/4" in stocking stitch /stockinette after blocking, knitted on the larger needle(s).

Key

A: Cornflower Blue
B: Powdered Egg
C: Ruby Red
D: Alabaster
MC: Nile Green
no stitch

Instructions

YOKE

Using crochet provisional method cast on 3 sts in the Colour A. Then, working with the larger needle(s) knit ____(A) rows of icord as follows:

Icord row: k3, return all 3 sts to the passive needle.

Break off the yarn, leaving a 30cm/12" tail. Place the 3 icord sts onto a safety pin.

Working with Colour B, pick up ____(A) sts through the nearest side of the sts along one st column of the icord. Join for working in the round, pm, then knit 17 rounds of the colourwork pattern following the Yoke Chart and working the charted increases in Round 12. Slip the marker at the beginning of each round.

Continuing in MC, knit 2 rounds, then increase as follows:

Increase round: sm, k____(B), lib, [k____(C), lib] ____(D) times, k to end.

You should now have ____(E) sts.

Yoke Chart

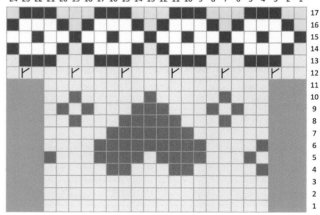

Size	32"	34"	36"	38"	40"	42"	44"	46"	48"	50"	52"	54"	56"	58"
A	162	180	180	180	198	198	198	198	216	216	216	234	234	252
B	13	30	10	6	17	11	9	6	36	12	6	39	14	42
C	10	60	20	12	33	22	13	11	72	24	12	78	19	84
D	19	3	11	19	7	11	19	23	3	11	23	3	15	3
E	236	244	252	260	272	276	284	288	292	300	312	316	328	340

FRONT NECK SHAPING

You will now work 'Japanese' short rows to drop the front neck. At the same time you will shape the sleevecaps as instructed to the right. Place the sleevecap markers and commence the short row shaping in the set-up rounds as follows:

Set-up Row 1 (RS): rm, k____(F), pm, k____(G), pm, k____(H), pm, k____(G), pm, [k to marker, sm] x2, k2, fasten safety pin around yarn, turn.

Set-up Row 2 (WS): sl1 purlwise wyif, [!][purl to marker, sm] x4, p2, fasten safety pin around yarn, turn.

Short Row 1 (RS): sl1 purlwise wyib, [!]k to gap of previous row turn (increasing as instructed for the sleevecaps), with loop and st after gap k2tog, k1, fasten safety pin around yarn, turn.

Short Row 2 (WS): sl1 purlwise wyif, [!]p to gap of previous row turn (slipping markers), with loop and st after gap ssp, p1, fasten safety pin around yarn, turn.

Work Short Rows 1 & 2 for a total of ____(I) rows.

Short Row 3 (RS): sl1 purlwise wyib, [!]k to gap of previous row turn (increasing as instructed for the sleevecaps), with loop and st after gap k2tog, k2, fasten safety pin around yarn, turn.

Short Row 4 (WS): sl1 purlwise wyif, [!]p to gap of previous row turn (slipping all markers), with loop and st after gap ssp, p2, fasten safety pin around yarn, turn.

Work Short Rows 3 & 4 for a total of ____(J) rows.

Completion Round Part 1: sl1 purlwise wyib, k to gap of previous row turn (increasing as instructed for the sleevecaps), with loop and st after gap k2tog.

Completion Round Part 2: k across front to 1 st before the gap, with loop and this st k2tog, pm. (End of round is now near centre front.)

[!]Always leave the safety pin on the yarn between the slipped st and the 1st st worked.

SLEEVECAPS

When you have completed a total of 25 rows from the icord at the top of the back neck, commence the sleevecap shaping. In every 2nd row/round (always on the RS), increase as follows until you have completed ____(K) increase rows/rounds:

Increase Row/Round 1: work an lia increase 1 st after the 1st and 3rd sleevecap markers, and work an lib increase 1 st before the 2nd and 4th sleevecap markers.

Then in every 2nd row/round (always on the RS), increase as follows until you have completed a further ____(L) increase rows/rounds:

> **Short Row Turns**
> With the safety pin you placed in the previous row, lift a loop of yarn onto the passive needle. Place the loop so it sits on the needle like a standard st. Remove safety pin. Work the loop and the next st together as stated, treating the loop as 1 st.

Size	32"	34"	36"	38"	40"	42"	44"	46"	48"	50"	52"	54"	56"	58"
F	46	47	49	50	52	53	54	54	55	56	58	59	61	63
G	26	28	28	30	32	32	34	36	36	38	40	40	42	44
H	92	94	98	100	104	106	108	108	110	112	116	118	122	126
I	30	30	32	32	34	34	34	34	36	36	38	38	40	40
J	6	6	6	6	6	6	6	6	6	6	6	6	6	8
K	19	18	19	18	18	18	17	15	15	14	13	13	13	12
L	4	6	6	8	9	10	12	14	15	17	18	19	20	21

Increase Row/Round 2: work an lib increase 1 st before *every* sleevecap marker, work an lia increase 1 st after *every* sleevecap marker.

Work one more round after the final increase round.

You should now have _____ (M) sts.

BODY

Set-up round 1: [knit to marker, rm, place sleevecap sts on waste yarn, then using crochet provisional method, cast on _____ (N) sts, rm] x2, k to end, sm.

You should now have _____ (O) sts.

Set-up round 2: [k to centre of provisional sts, pm] x2, k to end, sm.

Now knit 16 rounds in st-st, slipping each marker as you come to it.

Decrease as follows in the next, and every following 5th round until you have worked 10 decrease rounds in total.

Decrease round: [k to 2 sts before marker, k2tog, sm, skp] x2, k to end, sm.

You should now have _____ (P) sts.

Now knit 12 rounds in st-st, slipping all markers. You may adjust waist and overall length to fit by adding or removing rounds at this point.

Then increase as follows in the next, and every following 3rd round until you have worked 10 increase rounds in total.

Increase round: [k to 1 st before marker, lib, k1, sm, k1, lia] x2, k to end, sm.

You should now have _____ (O) sts.

Work a further 2 rounds without increasing.

Set up for the moss st (seed st) border as follows: remove the end of round marker, knit to 1 st before 1st side marker, lib, k1, sm. This will be the new end of round.

Change to smaller needle(s) and work 12 rounds of moss st (seed st), alternating the following 2 rounds:

Round 1: *k1, p1; rep from * to last st, k1.

Round 2: *p1, k1; rep from * to last st, p1.

Cast off loosely.

SLEEVES (both alike)

Join in MC, then with the larger needle(s) pick up and knit 1st plus the (N) provisional underarm sts, then the sleevecap sts from the waste yarn. Knit to the centre st of the provisional sts, pm.

You should have _____ (Q) sts on your needle(s).

Knit 6 rounds, then work a decrease round as follows:

Decrease round: k_____ (R), skp (S) times, k1, k2tog (S) times, k to end, sm.

You should now have _____ (T) sts.

Change to the smaller needle(s) and work 12 rounds of moss st (seed st) as for the bottom of the body.

Cast off loosely.

FINISHING

Neatly graft the reserved icord sts to the icord cast-on edge. Weave in all ends, then block to the dimensions shown in the diagram on the next page.

Size	32"	34"	36"	38"	40"	42"	44"	46"	48"	50"	52"	54"	56"	58"
M	344	364	376	396	416	428	448	460	472	492	508	520	540	556
N	2	4	6	6	6	10	10	14	16	18	18	20	22	24
O	204	220	232	244	256	272	284	300	312	328	340	352	368	384
P	164	180	192	204	216	232	244	260	272	288	300	312	328	344
Q	75	81	85	89	93	99	103	109	113	119	121	125	131	135
R	33	34	36	36	38	41	45	48	50	51	54	58	57	61
S	2	3	3	4	4	4	3	3	3	4	3	2	4	3
T	71	75	79	81	85	91	97	103	107	111	115	121	123	129

BLOCKING DIAGRAM

Neck edge circumference:
64 (70, 70, 70, 77, 77, 77, 77, 84, 84, 84, 91, 91, 98) cm
25 (28, 28, 28, 31, 31, 31, 31, 33, 33, 33, 36, 36, 39)"

Armhole depth:
18 (19, 20, 20, 22, 22, 23, 23,
24, 25, 25, 26, 27, 27) cm
7 (8, 8, 8, 9, 9, 9, 9, 10, 10, 10,
10, 11, 11)"

Sleeve circumference at underarm:
29 (32, 33, 35, 36, 39, 40,
43, 44, 46, 47, 49, 51, 53)
cm
12 (13, 13, 14, 14, 15, 16,
17, 18, 18, 19, 19, 20, 21)"

Chest circumference:
81 (86, 91, 97, 102, 107, 112, 119,
122, 130, 135, 140, 145, 152) cm
32 (34, 36, 38, 40, 42, 44, 47, 48,
51, 53, 55, 57, 60)"

Length:
54 (55, 56, 57, 58, 58, 59, 60,
60, 61, 62, 62, 63, 64) cm
21 (22, 22, 22, 23, 23, 23, 24,
24, 24, 24, 25, 25, 25)"

Waist circumference:
64 (70, 75, 80, 84, 91, 95, 102, 106,
112,117, 122, 128, 135) cm
25¼ (27¾, 29½, 31½, 33¼, 35¾,
37½, 40, 41¾, 44¼, 46¼, 48, 50½,
53)"

Hip circumference:
81 (86, 91, 97, 102, 107, 112, 119, 122,
130, 135, 140, 145, 152) cm
32 (34, 36, 38, 40, 42, 44, 47, 48, 51, 53,
55, 57, 60)"

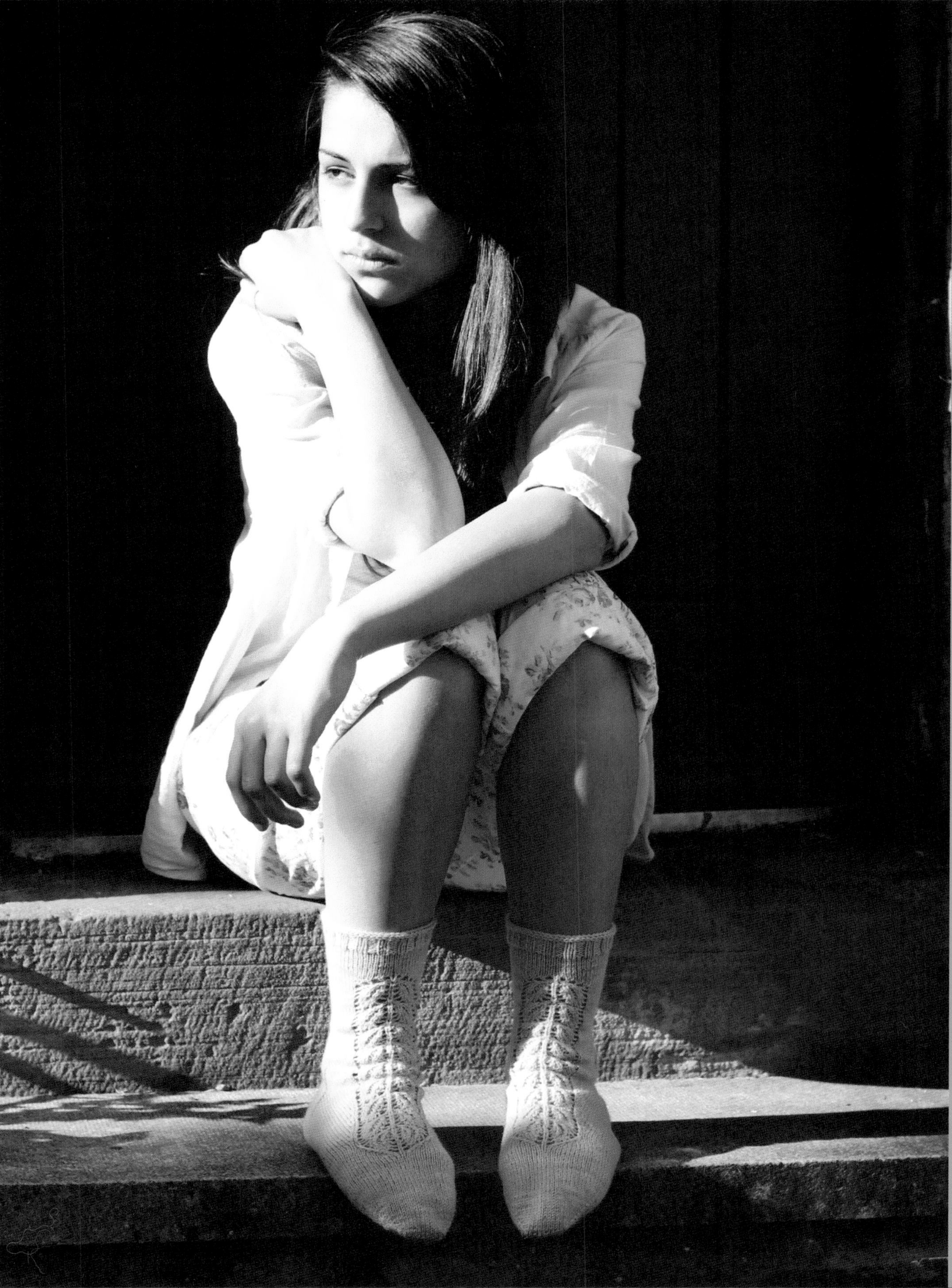

SIZE

20½(23:25½)cm/8(9:10)" foot circumferences. Foot length is customised.

MATERIALS

75g of any 4ply/fingering weight sock yarn with approximately 400 metres per 100g. The socks pictured were knitted with 'Rockhopper' from Literally Yarn.

NEEDLES AND NOTIONS

Appropriate 2.75mm/US 2 needles (or size required to get the specified tension/gauge) for your preferred method of small diameter circular knitting; DPNs, or two 60cm/24" long circulars, or one long circular (80cm/32" or longer) for the magic loop method.

4 stitchmarkers

A darning needle

TENSION/GAUGE

34 sts and 48 rounds per 10cm/4" in stocking stitch/ stockinette knitted in the round.

Instructions

TOE

Using Judy's magic cast-on or Turkish cast-on method, cast 7(9:11) sts onto each of two needles. *14(18:22) sts*

Working in rounds increase as follows:

Round 1: knit

Round 2: k1, lib, k to 1 st before centre of round, lia, k2, lib, k to 1 st before end of round, lia, k1.

Repeat these 2 rounds until you have increased to 62(70:78) sts.

Now knit without further increasing until the toe measures 8(9:10)cm/3(3½:4)" from the end.

INSTEP

Set-up round: k7(9:11), pm, k17, pm, k to end.

Lace Panel beginning:

Work on the 17 sts between stitch-markers as instructed below, or as charted on next page. Work all other sts in st-st.

Round 1: sm, k6, k2tog, yo, k1, yo, skp, k6, sm.

Rounds 2, 4, and 6: knit

Round 3: sm, k4, k3tog, [yo, k1] x3, yo, s2kp, k4, sm.

Round 5: sm, k2, k3tog, yo, k3, yo, k1, yo, k3, yo, s2kp, k2, sm.

Round 7: rm, k3tog, pm, yo, k5, yo, k1, yo, k5, yo, pm, s2kp, rm.

Lace Panel repeat:

Work on the sts between stitch-markers as instructed below, or as charted on next page. Work all other sts in st-st, increasing for the arch as instructed in the arch expansion section.

Rounds 1 and 9: knit

Rounds 2 and 4: sm, **yo, k1, k2tog, p1, skp, k1, yo,** k1, rep from ** to **, sm.

Rounds 3 and 5: sm, k3, p1, k7, p1, k3, sm.

Round 6: sm, yo, k1, yo, k2tog, p1, s2kp, yo, k1, yo, k3tog, p1, skp, yo, k1, yo, sm.

Round 7: sm, k4, p1, k5, p1, k4, sm.

Round 8: sm, yo, k3, yo, s3kp, k1, k4tog, yo, k3, yo, sm.

Round 10: yo, k5, yo, cdd, yo, k5, yo, sm.

Repeat these 10 rounds for the remainder of the instep and leg until instructed to end the lace panel.

!There are 2 sts less than the stated st count after a row 8 or 9 of the lace panel.

LACE PANEL BEGINNING

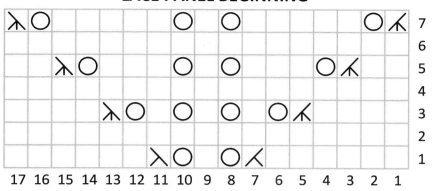

LACE PANEL REPEAT

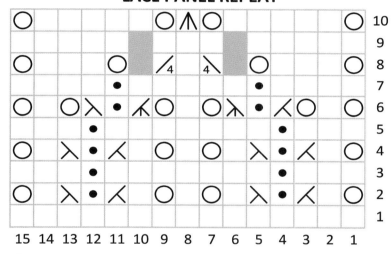

!There are 2 sts less than the stated st count after a row 8 or 9 of the lace panel.

LACE PANEL ENDING

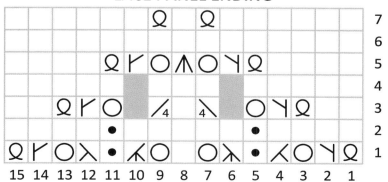

ARCH EXPANSION

Commence the arch increases as follows when the sock measures 15(17:19)cm/6(6¾:7½)" less than the total desired foot length.

Round 1: k to 1 st before the lace panel, lia, k1, sm, knit lace panel as previously instructed, sm, k1, lib, k to end.

Rounds 2 and 3: knit to marker, sm, knit lace panel as previously instructed, sm, k to end.

Repeat these 3 rounds until you have worked them 15(17:19) times in total. *92(104:116) sts* [!]

SHAPE HEEL

Set-up row 1: k to marker, sm, knit lace panel as previously instructed, sm, k37(43:49), sl1 purlwise wyib, turn.

Set-up row 2: sl1 purlwise wyib, p27(31:35), sl1 purlwise wyif, turn.

Short Row 1: sl1 purlwise wyif, k to 1 st before wrapped st of last row, sl1 purlwise wyib, turn.

Short Row 2: sl1 purlwise wyib, p to 1 st before wrapped st of last row, sl1 purlwise wyif, turn.

Repeat Short Rows 1 and 2 until you have worked them 7(8:9) times in total.

Next Row: sl1 purlwise wyif, k to 1st wrapped st, [knit together the wrap and the st it wraps] 7(8:9) times. Then from in front insert the working needle into the next wrap and st it wraps and lift them off the passive needle, knit the next st, then pass the wrap and the slipped st over it. Turn.

Next Row: sl1 purlwise wyif, p to 1st wrapped st, [purl together the wrap and the st it wraps] 7(8:9) times. Then from behind insert the working needle into the next wrap and st it wraps and lift them off the passive needle, purl the next st, then pass the wrap and the slipped st over it. Turn. *90(102:114) sts* [!]

TURN HEEL

Row 1: sl1 purlwise wyib, k to 1 st before the turn of the previous row, skp, turn.

Row 2: sl1 purlwise wyif, p to 1 st before turn of the previous row, p2tog, turn.

Repeat Rows 1 and 2 until you have worked them a total of 13(15:17) times.

Final row: sl1 purlwise wyib, k27(31:35), skp, k to marker, sm, knit lace panel as previously instructed, sm, k9(11:13), k2tog, k28(32:36). *62(70:78) sts* [!]

[!] There are 2 sts less than the stated st count after a row 8 or 9 of the lace panel.

LEG

Work in rounds, continuing the lace panel as established. Work all other sts in st-st until the start of the next round containing a Row 3 of the lace panel repeat. In this round work as follows:

Set-up Round: k to marker, sm, knit lace panel as previously instructed, sm, k15(19:23), pm, k17, pm, k to end.

In the next 7 rounds continue the front lace panel as established, and follow the 'Lace Panel beginning' instructions (see page 2) for the 17 sts between the 2nd pair of stitchmarkers. Work the sts between the two lace panels in st-st.

In the following 15 rounds work the 'Lace Panel repeat' on both the front and the back lace panels, stopping after a Round 5 of the repeat. Then close both panels as instructed below.

Lace Panel ending:

Work on the lace panel sts between each pair of stitch-markers as charted on page 13, or as instructed on the next page. Work all other sts in st-st.

Round 1: sm, k1b, lia, yo, k2tog, p1, s2kp, yo, k1, yo, k3tog, p1, skp, yo, lib, k1b, sm.

Round 2: sm, k4, p1, k5, p1, k4, sm.

Round 3: k2, k1b, lia, yo, s3kp, k1, k4tog, yo, lib, k1b, k2, sm.

Round 4: sm, k13, sm.

Round 5: sm, k4, k1b, lia, yo, cdd, yo, lib, k1b, k4, sm.

Round 6: sm, k15, sm.

Round 7: rm, k6, k1b, k1, k1b, k6, rm.

Now knit 10 rounds in st-st before working the cuff.

CUFF

Set-up Round: *lib, k1, [p2, k2] 7(8:9) times, p2; rep from * to end. *64(72:80) sts*

Rounds 1-8: *k2, p2; rep from * to end.

Now work a 3-st applied icord cast-off as follows:

Knit 2, skp, return 3 sts to passive needle; rep from * until all cuff sts have been cast off. Break off the yarn leaving a 20cm/8" tail and use this to graft the remaining sts to the icord beginning.

FINISHING

Weave in all ends then block - either soak and stretch the socks on sock blockers until dry, or press them under a damp cloth with a warm iron.

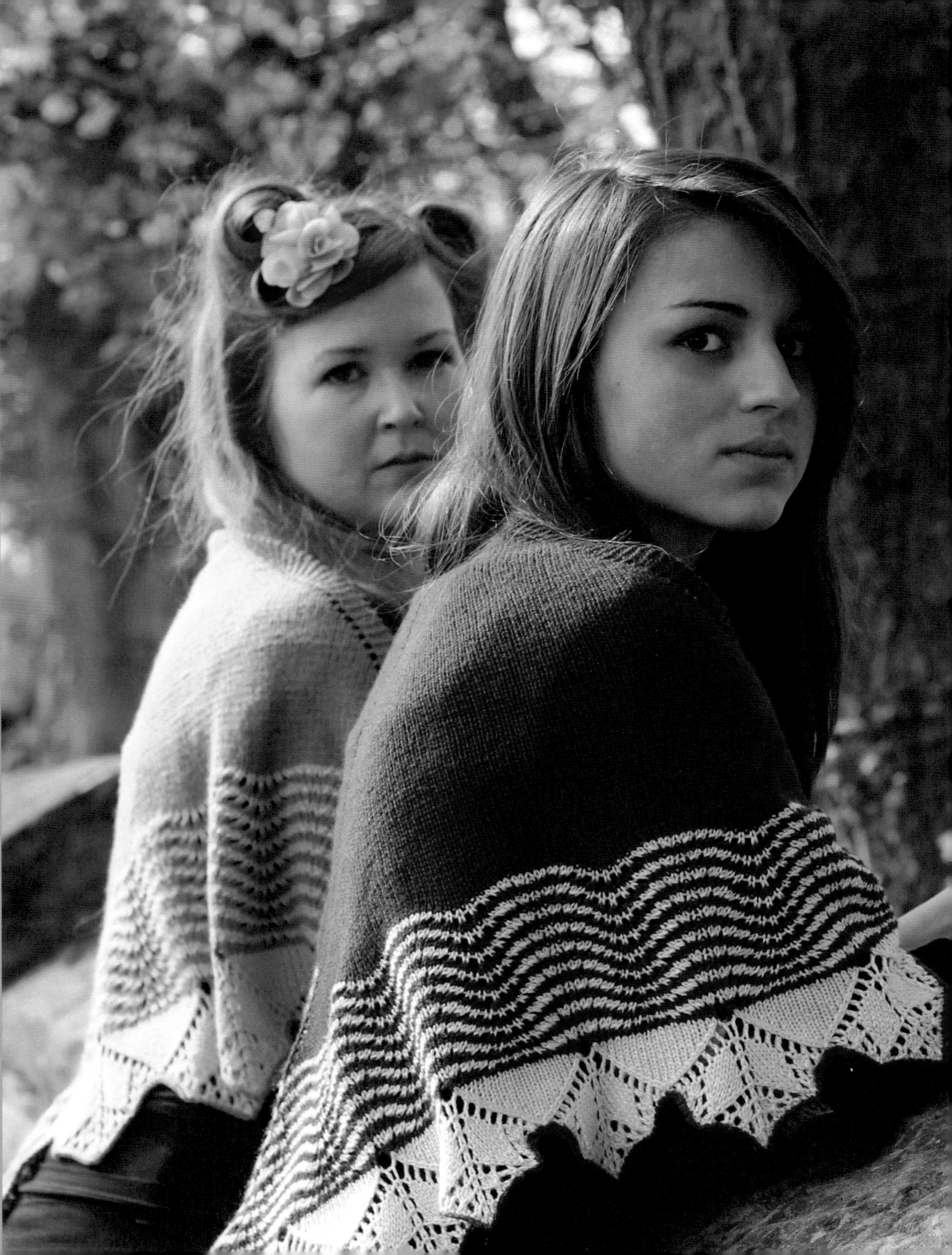

SIZE

After blocking both versions are 127cm/50" wide at the top edge and 71cm/28" deep at the centre back.

MATERIALS

Any even sportweight or DK yarn in two solid colours.

For the DK version you will need aproximately 330 metres (361 yards) of main colour and 220 metres (241 yards) of contrast colour.

For the sportweight version you will need approximately 360 metres (394 yards) of the main colour, and 240 metres (262 yards) of contrast colour.

The blue sample was knitted in Debbie Bliss 'Cashmerino DK' in shades #44 and #46.

The red sample was knitted in 'Scrumptious 4ply Sport' (55% merino 45% silk) from Fyberspates in Cherry and Baby Pink.

NEEDLES

A 100cm/36" long 4mm /US 6 circular needle for the DK version.

A 100cm/36" long 3.75mm /US 5 circular needle for the sportweight version.

TENSION/GAUGE

DK version: 20 sts and 28 rows per 10cm/4" in blocked stocking stitch/stockinette.

Sportweight version: 22 sts and 36 rows per 10cm/4" in blocked stocking stitch/stockinette.

Instructions

Where two options appear please follow the first numbers for the DK version, and the second numbers (in round parentheses) for the sportweight version.

MAIN SECTION

Leaving a 30cm/12" tail cast on 11 sts in MC with the crochet provisional method. Proceed as follows:

Row 1: k5, yo, k1, yo, k5. *(13 sts)*

Row 2: k5, p3, k5.

Row 3: k5, [yo, k1] x4, k4. *(17 sts)*

Row 4: k5, p7, k5.

Row 5: k5, yo, k3, yo, k1, yo, k3, yo, k5. *(21 sts)*

Row 6 and all following even-numbered rows: k5, p to the last 5 sts, k5.

Row 7 and all following odd-numbered rows: k5, yo, k to the centre st, yo, k1, yo, k to the last 5 sts, yo, k5.

Repeat rows 6 and 7 above until there are a total of 189(225) sts on your needle following a Row 6.

Leaving MC attached, join in CC and work one repeat of Row 7 and Row 6 in CC before commencing the feather and fan pattern as instructed on the next page. You should now have 193(229) sts on your needle.

FEATHER AND FAN STRIPE

Row 1: In MC k5, yo, **k1, k2tog x3, [yo, k1] x5, yo, skp x3.** Repeat from ** to ** 4(5) times more, [k1, yo] x2. Then repeat from ** to ** 5(6) times, k1, yo, k5. *197(233) sts*

Rows 2, 6, 10, 14, 18, 22, 26, 30 and 34: In MC k5, purl to the last 5 sts, k5.

Rows 3, 7, 11, 15, 19, 23, 27, and 31: In CC k5, yo, k to the centre st, yo, k1, yo, k to the last 5 sts, yo, k5.

Rows 4, 8, 12, 16, 20, 24, 28, and 32: In CC k5, purl to the last 5 sts, k5.

Row 5: In MC k5, yo, k2, **k1, k2tog x3, [yo, k1] x5, yo, skp x3.** Repeat from ** to ** 4(5) times more, k3, [yo, k1] x2, k1. Then repeat from ** to ** 5(6) times, k3, yo, k5. *205(241) sts*

Row 9: In MC k5, yo, k2, yo, skp, **k1, k2tog x3, [yo, k1] x5, yo, skp x3.** Repeat from ** to ** 4(5) times more, k1, k2tog, yo, k2, yo, k1, yo, k2, yo skp. Then repeat from ** to ** 5(6) times, k1, k2tog, yo, k2, yo, k5. *213(249) sts*

Row 13: In MC k5, yo, k1, k2tog, yo, k1, yo, skp, **k1, k2tog x3, [yo, k1] x5, yo, skp x3.** Repeat from ** to ** 4(5) times more, k1, k2tog, yo, k1, yo, skp, [k1, yo] x2, k1, k2tog, yo, k1, yo, skp. Then repeat from ** to ** 5(6) times, k1, k2tog, yo, k1, yo, skp, k1, yo, k5. *221(257) sts*

Charts for the feather and fan stripes

RS rows: k5, **work across Chart A once, Chart B 5(6) times, and chart C once.** Knit the centre stitch, repeat from ** to **, then k5.

For Chart B follow line 1 on all RS rows where you are working in MC, and follow line 3 on all RS rows where you are working in CC.

WS rows: in the same colour as the previous row k5, p to the last 5 sts, k5.

Chart A

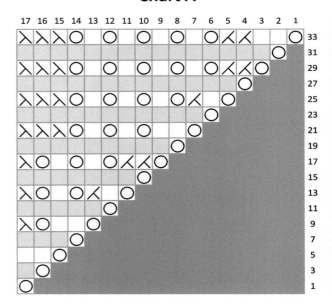

Chart B

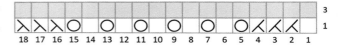

Chart C

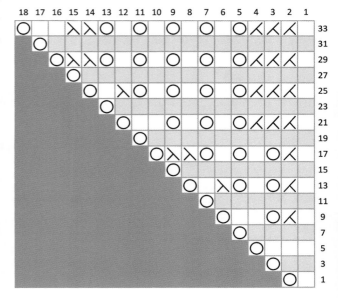

Row 17: In MC k5, yo, k2tog x2, [yo, k1] x2, yo, skp, **k1, k2tog x3, [yo, k1] x5, yo, skp x3.** Repeat from ** to ** 4(5) times more, k1, k2tog, [yo, k1] x2, yo, skp x2, yo, k1, yo, k2tog x2, [yo, k1] x2, yo, skp. Then repeat from ** to ** 5(6) times, k1, k2tog, [yo, k1] x2, yo, skp x2, yo, k5. *229(265)sts*

Row 21: In MC k5, yo, k2, [yo, k1] x2, yo, skp x3, **k1, k2tog x3, [yo, k1] x5, yo, skp x3.** Repeat from ** to ** 4(5) times more, k1, k2tog x3, [yo, k1] x3, [k1, yo] x2, k1, [k1, yo] x3, skp x3. Then repeat from ** to ** 5(6) times, k1, k2tog x3, [yo, k1] x3, k1, yo, k5. *237(273) sts*

Row 25: In MC k5, yo, k1, k2tog, [yo, k1] x3, yo, skp x3, **k1, k2tog x3, [yo, k1] x5, yo, skp x3.** Repeat from ** to ** 4(5) times more, k1, k2tog x3, [yo, k1] x3, yo, skp, [k1, yo] x2, k1, k2tog, [yo, k1] x3, yo, skp x3. Then repeat from ** to ** 5(6) times, k1, k2tog x3, [yo, k1] x3, yo, skp, k1, yo, k5. *245(281) sts*

Row 29: In MC yo, k2tog x2, [yo, k1] x4, yo, skp x3, **k1, k2tog x3, [yo, k1] x5, yo, skp x3.** Repeat from ** to ** 4(5) times more, k1, k3tog x3, [yo, k1] x4, yo, skp x2, yo, k1, yo, k2tog x2, [yo, k1] x4, yo, skp x3. Then repeat from ** to ** 5(6) times, k1, k3tog x3, [yo, k1] x4, yo, skp x2, yo, k5. *253(289) sts*

Row 33: In MC k5, yo, k2, k2tog x2, [yo, k1] x4, yo, skp x3, **k1, k2tog x3, [yo, k1] x5, yo, skp x3.** Repeat from ** to ** 4(5) times more, k1, k2tog x3, [yo, k1] x4, yo, skp x2, k2, [yo, k1] x2, k1, k2tog x2, [yo, k1] x4, yo, skp x3. Then repeat from ** to ** 5(6) times, k1, k2tog x3, [yo, k1] x4, yo, skp x2, k2, yo, k5. *261(297) sts*

After completing Row 34 break off the MC yarn leaving a short tail for weaving in later.

Chart D

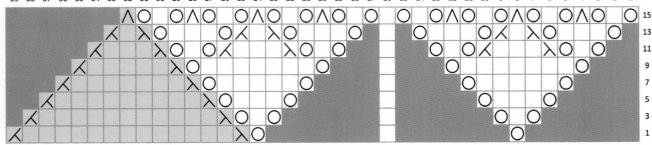

Chart for the lace edging

Work the set-up rows first (see written instructions below), then continue as follows:

RS rows: k5, **work across Chart D 8(9) times, omitting the sts highlighted yellow in the final repeat,** knit the centre stitch, repeat from ** to **, then k5.

WS rows: k5, p to the last 5 sts, k5.

LACE EDGING

Continuing with CC only, work the edging as follows:

Set-up row 1: k5, yo, k1, **k16, yo, skp.** Repeat from ** to ** 5(6) times more, k16, [yo, k1] x2. Then repeat from ** to ** 6(7) times, k16, yo, k5. *265(301) sts*

Set-up row 2 and all even-numbered rows: k5, p to the last 5 sts, k5.

Row 1: k5, **yo, k1, yo, skp, k13, k2tog.** Repeat from ** to ** 6(7) times more, [yo, k1] x2. Then repeat from ** to ** 7(8) times, [yo, k1] x2, k4. *269(305) sts*

Row 3: k5, **[yo, k1] x3, yo, skp, k11, k2tog.** Repeat from ** to ** 6(7) times more, [yo, k1] x4. Then repeat from ** to ** 7(8) times, [yo, k1] x4, k4. *305(345) sts*

Row 5: k5, **yo, k3, yo, k1, yo, k3, yo, skp, k9, k2tog.** Repeat from ** to ** 6(7) times more, [yo, k3, yo, k1] x2. Then repeat from ** to ** 7(8) times, [yo, k3, yo, k1] x2, k4. *341(385) sts*

Row 7: k5, **yo, k5, yo, k1, yo, k5, yo, skp, k7, k2tog.** Repeat from ** to ** 6(7) times more, [yo, k5, yo, k1] x2. Then repeat from ** to ** 7(8) times, [yo, k5, yo, k1] x2, k4. *377(425) sts*

Row 9: k5, **yo, k7, yo, k1, yo, k7, yo, skp, k5, k2tog.** Repeat from ** to ** 6(7) times more, [yo, k7, yo, k1] x2. Then repeat from ** to ** 7(8) times, [yo, k7, yo, k1] x2, k4. *413(465) sts*

Row 11: k5, **yo, k1, yo, skp, k3, k2tog, [yo, k1] x3, yo, skp, k3, k2tog, yo, k1, yo, skp, k3, k2tog** Repeat from ** to ** 6(7) times more, yo, k1, yo, skp, k3, k2tog, [yo, k1] x3, yo, skp, k3, k2tog, [yo, k1] x2. Then repeat from ** to ** 7(8) times, yo, k1, yo, skp, k3, k2tog, [yo, k1] x3, yo, skp, k3, k2tog, [yo, k1] x2, k4. *449(505) sts*

Row 13: k5, **yo, k3, yo, skp, k1, k2tog, yo, k3, yo, k1, [yo, k3, yo, skp, k1, k2tog] x2.** Repeat from ** to ** 6(7) times more, yo, k3, yo, skp, k1, k2tog, yo, k3, yo, k1, yo, k3, yo, skp, k1, k2tog, yo, k3, yo, k1. Then repeat from ** to ** 7(8) times, yo, k3, yo, skp, k1, k2tog, yo, k3, yo, k1, yo, k3, yo, skp, k1, k2tog, yo, k3, yo, k5. *485(545) sts*

Row 15: k5, **yo, k1, [yo, sk2p, yo, k1] x3, yo, k1, [yo, k1, yo, sk2p] x4.** Repeat from ** to ** 6(7) times more, yo, k1, [yo, sk2p, yo, k1] x3, yo, k1, [yo, k1, yo, sk2p] x3, [yo, k1] x2. Then repeat from ** to ** 7(8) times, yo, k1, [yo, sk2p, yo, k1] x3, yo, k1, [yo, k1, yo, sk2p] x3, [yo, k1] x2, k4. *521(585) sts*

After working Row 16 (WS) break off the CC yarn leaving a short tail for weaving in later.

Join in the MC yarn and cast (bind) off as follows:

K1, *sl1 knitwise, return both sts to the passive needle (with reversed mount) then k them together tbl. Repeat from * until all sts have been cast (bound) off. Break off the MC yarn leaving a short tail, and pull this through the final st.

FINISHING

Pick up 10 sts from the cast-on. With the tail from the cast-on purl the first 5 sts, finishing in the middle of the row. Hold the sts just purled and the remaining 5 sts on separate needles ready for grafting. Thread the remainder of the tail onto a darning needle, then use it to graft the 2 sets of sts together in garter st as follows:

Hold the needles together with the right sides of the knitting facing outwards. The tail of yarn should be coming from the first st on the back needle.

Take the yarn through the first st on both the front and back needles knitwise. Then, starting at the front needle *take the yarn through the first st on the needle purlwise and take the st off the needle. Take the yarn through the next st knitwise and leave it on the needle. Change to the other needle. Repeat from * until all sts have been worked. Finally take the darning needle through the last st on each needle purlwise, taking each st off the needle as you do so.

Weave in all yarn ends then block the shawl. Soak it in lukewarm water until thoroughly damp, then pin it out to the measurements given on page 17. Carefully pin out the points of the lace edging to the shapes shown in the pictured samples. Leave the shawl to dry, then unpin and enjoy it!

Summer afternoon—summer afternoon; to me those have always been the two most beautiful words in the English language. ~Henry James

To knitters summer is the season of lace. Wonderfully fine, light, airy and delicate, intricate knitted lace is justly viewed by many as the pinnacle of achievement in our craft.

The three lace designs pictured here feature another of my favourite fibres. Silk spins into cool yarn with luxurious sheen and slinky drape, making it an ideal choice for summer knits. As a natural fibre it responds well to blocking, revealing the full glory of lace patterns.

The designs are also great for special events. A light summer cardigan for your summer holiday, a beautiful pair of evening gloves for a concert or dance, and a fine lace stole to wear at a wedding or to gift to the bride.

Glade

Prom

Summer Seas

Glade

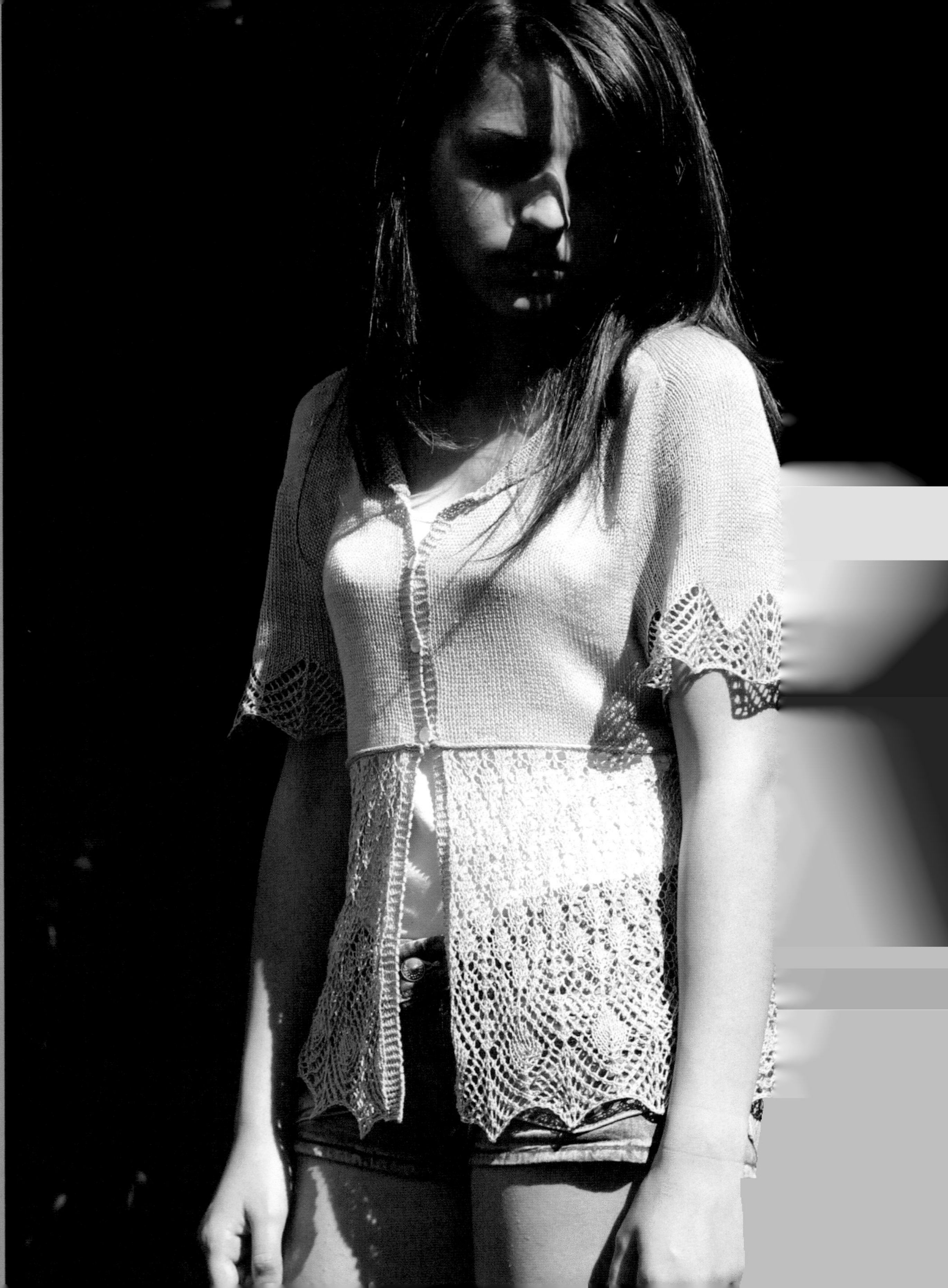

Instructions

SHOULDERS

Using a provisional method, cast on ____(A) sts with the larger needle(s).

Rows 1–6: knit

Row 7 (RS): knit to the last 5 sts, k2tog, yo, k3.

Rows 8–11: knit

Row 12 (WS): k6, p to last 6 sts, k6.

Place shoulder markers and commence short row front neck and shoulder shaping as follows:

Short Row 1: k____(B) sts, m1b, pm, k____(C) sts, pm, m1f, k____(D) sts, m1b, pm, k____(C) sts, pm, m1f, sl1 purlwise wyib, turn.

Short Row 2: sl1 purlwise wyib, [p to marker, m1fp, sm, p to marker, sm, m1bp] x2, p1, sl1 purlwise wyif, turn.

Short Row 3: sl1 purlwise wyif, [k to marker, m1b, sm, k to marker, sm, m1f] x2, k to wrapped st of previous row, k together wrap with the st it wraps, sl1 purlwise wyib, turn.

Short Row 4: sl1 purlwise wyib, [p to marker, m1fp, sm, p to marker, sm, m1bp] x2, p to wrapped st of previous row, p together wrap with the st it wraps, sl1 purlwise wyif, turn.

Work Short Rows 3 and 4 for a total of ____(E) rows. This completes the shoulder increases.

You should now have ____(F) sts in total, including the sts outside the short rows.

SIZE
To fit 32(34:36:38:40:42:44:46:48:50:52:54:56:58)" chest with 2–3" of positive ease.

MATERIALS
2ply/laceweight silk yarn with approximately 750 metres /820 yards per 100g. You will need 1(2:2:2:2:2:2:2:2:2: 2:2:2:2) 100g skeins.

The pictured sample was knitted with Natural Dye Studio 'Spyder Silk' in the 'Evergreen Glade' shade.

NEEDLES AND NOTIONS
2.75mm/US 2 and 3mm/US 2½ needles for your preferred methods of small diameter circular knitting and flat knitting with long rows.

Adjust needle size as necessary to achieve the specified tensions.

Four stitchmarkers. Five 8mm/⅓" buttons

TENSION/GAUGE
28 sts and 36 rows per 10cm/4" in stocking stitch /stockinette after blocking, knitted on the larger needle(s).

SLEEVECAPS

Work sleevecap increases in the next ____(G) rows as follows. At the same time continue the front neck shaping and buttonhole shaping (see next page).

RS increase rows: work an m1f increase immediately after the 1st and 3rd markers. Work an m1b increase immediately before the 2nd and 4th markers.

WS increase rows A: work an m1bp increase immediately after the 1st and 3rd markers. Work an m1fp increase immediately before the 2nd and 4th markers.

Size	32"	34"	36"	38"	40"	42"	44"	46"	48"	50"	52"	54"	56"	58"
A	178	188	198	198	208	216	222	230	236	238	250	260	272	278
B	32	34	36	35	37	38	39	40	41	41	43	45	47	48
C	28	29	30	32	33	35	36	38	39	40	42	43	45	46
D	58	62	66	64	68	70	72	74	76	76	80	84	88	90
E	18	18	18	20	20	20	20	20	20	20	20	20	20	20
F	258	268	278	286	296	304	310	318	324	326	338	348	360	366
G	6	6	6	6	8	8	8	8	8	8	10	10	10	10

Then increase in the next and every following 4th row ____(H) times, ending after a WS row.

Then increase in every RS row and every WS row for a total of ____(I) rows, working the RS rows as above and the WS rows as follows:

WS increase rows B: work an mifp increase 1 st before the 1st and 3rd markers. Work an m1bp increase 1 st after the 2nd and 4th markers.

You should now have ____(J) sts in total.

FRONT NECK SHAPING

At the same time a working the sleevecap shaping, continue to shape the front neck as follows:

Short Row 1 (RS): sl1 purlwise wyif, work to the wrapped st of the previous RS row, k together wrap with the st it wraps, sl1 purlwise wyib, turn.

Short Row 2 (WS): sl1 purlwise wyib, work to the wrapped st of the previous purl row, p together wrap with the st it wraps, sl1 purlwise wyif, turn.

Work Short Rows 1 and 2 for a total of ____(K) rows.

Work the following short rows once only:

Short Row 3 (RS): sl1 purlwise wyif, work to the wrapped st of the previous RS row, k together wrap with the st it wraps, k1, sl1 purlwise wyib, turn.

Short Row 4 (WS): sl1 purlwise wyib, work to the wrapped st of the previous purl row, p together wrap with the st it wraps, p1, sl1 purlwise wyif, turn.

Short Row 5 (RS): sl1 purlwise wyif, work to the wrapped st of the previous RS row, k together wrap with the st it wraps, k2, sl1 purlwise wyib, turn.

Short Row 6 (WS): sl1 purlwise wyib, work to the wrapped st of the previous purl row, p together wrap with the st it wraps, p2, sl1 purlwise wyif, turn.

Final RS Short Row: sl1 purlwise wyif, work to the wrapped st of the previous RS row, k together wrap with the st it wraps, k to end.

Final WS Short Row: k6, work to the wrapped st of the previous purl row, p together wrap with the st it wraps, p to last 6 sts, k6.

BUTTONHOLES

After completing the short row neck shaping, k the first 6 and last 6 sts in WS rows, purling all other WS row sts.

There are 5 buttonholes in total, including the buttonhole in Row 7 of the shoulder instructions.

Counting rows from the buttonhole worked in Row 7 of the shoulder instructions, place buttonholes at the end of every ____(L) rows as follows:

Buttonhole Row: Work to the last 5 sts, k2tog, yo, k3.

Size	32"	34"	36"	38"	40"	42"	44"	46"	48"	50"	52"	54"	56"	58"
H	8	7	7	6	6	6	5	4	4	4	3	2	2	1
I	12	16	18	22	24	26	30	34	38	42	44	48	50	54
J	338	352	366	378	400	412	422	434	448	458	478	492	508	518
K	6	6	8	6	8	10	10	10	12	14	14	14	16	16
L	16th	16th	16th	18th	18th	18th	18th	18th	18th	18th	18th	18th	18th	18th

LOWER BODICE

When you have completed the sleevecaps, remove the sleeve sts and commence side decreases as follows:

Row 1 (RS): [k to marker, rm, place sleeve sts on waste yarn, using a provisional method cast on _____(M) sts immediately next to the last st worked, rm] x2, k to end.

You should now have _____(N) sts on the needle(s).

Row 2 (WS): [p to centre point of the provisional underarm sts, pm] x2, p to end.

Decrease as follows in the next row, and then in every 4th row until you have worked the decrease row 7 times in total:

Decrease Row: [k to 2 sts before marker, k2tog, sm, skp] x2, k to end.

When all the decrease rounds have been completed you should have _____(O) sts on the needle(s).

Work a further 2 rows, ending with a RS row. Then, continuing with the larger needle(s), work an applied icord from the WS as follows:

Cast on 3 sts next to the first st on the WS row (ie the last st worked), then *k2, skp, return 3 sts to the passive needle; rep from * until all the bodice sts have been worked. Cast off (bind off) the 3 icord sts, leaving the final st from the cast-off on the needle.

SKIRT

Using the smaller needle(s), pick up and knit one st for each row of icord, picking up from the edge of the icord that is nearest to the WS. Pass the st from the cast-off over the first new st.

You should now have _____(O) sts on your needle.

Set-up row (WS): p _____(P) sts, m1bp, *p _____(Q) sts, m1bp; rep from * to last _____(P) sts, p to end.

You should now have _____(R) sts on the needle.

Now work the lace pattern as follows:

Row 1: k7, *k2, yo, sk2p, yo, k3; rep from * to last 6 sts, k6.

Row 2 and all even-numbered rows: k6, p to last 6 sts, k6.

Row 3: k6, k2tog, *k2, yo, k1, yo, k2, sk2p; rep from * to last 13 sts, k2, yo, k1, yo, k2, skp, k6.

Row 5: k6, k2tog, *k1, yo, k3, yo, k1, sk2p; rep from * to last 13 sts, k1, yo, k3, yo, k1, skp, k6.

Row 7: k6, k2tog, *yo, k5, yo, sk2p; rep from * to last 13 sts, yo, k5, yo, skp, k6.

Row 9: k7, *yo, k2, sk2p, k2, yo, k1; rep from * to last 6 sts, k6.

Row 11: k7, *k1, yo, k1, sk2p, k1, yo, k2; rep from * to last 6 sts, k6.

Size	32"	34"	36"	38"	40"	42"	44"	46"	48"	50"	52"	54"	56"	58"
M	10	10	12	12	12	14	18	20	20	22	22	22	24	26
N	246	262	278	290	302	314	334	350	362	374	386	402	418	434
O	218	234	250	262	274	286	306	322	334	346	358	374	390	406
P	10	9	8	20	17	10	18	16	13	11	26	28	30	29
Q	11	12	13	37	24	19	27	29	22	18	51	53	55	58
R	237	253	269	269	285	301	317	333	349	365	365	381	397	413

Rows 1–12 form the leaf lace repeat. Work through the repeat for a total of 48 rows.

Row 13: k7, *k2, [yo, sk2p, yo, k1b] x2, yo, sk2p, yo, k3; rep from * to last 6 sts, k6.

Row 15: k6, k2tog, *[k2, yo] x2, skp, k1, k2tog, [yo, k2] x2, sk2p; rep from * to last 21 sts, [k2, yo] x2, skp, k1, k2tog, [yo, k2] x2, skp, k6.

Row 17: k6, k2tog, *k1, yo, k2, yo, skp, yo, sk2p, yo, k2tog, yo, k2, yo, k1, sk2p; rep from * to last 21 sts, k1, yo, k2, yo, skp, yo, sk2p, yo, k2tog, yo, k2, yo, k1, skp, k6.

Row 19: k6, k2tog, *yo, k2, [yo, skp] x2, k1, [k2tog, yo] x2, k2, yo, sk2p; rep from * to last 21 sts, yo, k2, [yo, skp] x2, k1, [k2tog, yo] x2, k2, yo, skp, k6.

Row 21: k7, *[yo, skp] x3, yo sk2p, yo, [k2tog, yo] x3, k1; rep from * to last 6 sts, k6.

Row 23: k7, *k1, [yo, skp] x3, k1, [k2tog, yo] x3, k2; rep from * to last 6 sts, k6.

Row 25: as Row 21.

Row 27: as Row 23.

Row 29: k7, *k2, [yo, skp] x2, yo, sk2p, yo, [k2tog, yo] x2, k3; rep from * to last 6 sts, k6.

Row 31: k7, *k3, [yo, skp] x2, k1, [k2tog, yo] x2, k4; rep from * to last 6 sts, k6.

Row 33: k7, *k4, yo, skp, yo sk2p, yo, k2tog, yo, k5; rep from * to last 6 sts, k6.

Row 35: k6, k2tog, *k3, yo, k2tog, yo, k3, yo, skp, yo, k3, sk2p; rep from * to last 21 sts, k3, yo, k2tog, yo, k3, yo, skp, yo, k3, skp, k6.

Row 37: k6, k2tog, *k2, [yo, k2tog] x2, yo, k1, yo, [skp, yo] x2, k2, sk2p; rep from * to last 21 sts, k2, [yo, k2tog] x2, yo, k1, yo, [skp, yo] x2, k2, skp, k6.

Row 39: k6, k2tog, *k1, [yo, k2tog] x2, yo, k3, yo, [skp, yo] x2, k1, sk2p; rep from * to last 21 sts, k1, [yo, k2tog] x2, yo, k3, yo, [skp, yo] x2, k1, skp, k6.

Row 41: k6, k2tog, *[yo, k2tog] x3, yo, k1, yo, [skp, yo] x3, sk2p; rep from * to last 21 sts, [yo, k2tog] x3, yo, k1, yo, [skp, yo] x3, skp, k6.

Row 43: k7, *[k2tog, yo] x3, k3, [yo, skp] x3, k1; rep from * to last 6 sts, k6.

Row 45: as Row 41.

Row 47: as Row 43.

Row 49: as Row 41.

Row 50: k6, p to last 6 sts, k6.

Using the larger needle(s), cast off (bind off) *very loosely* as follows: k1, *sl1 knitwise, return 2 sts to the passive needle, k2tog tbl; rep from * to end.

SLEEVES (both alike)

Using the smaller needle, pick up and knit the reserved sts from the waste yarn, and the provisional sts from the underarm, placing a marker after the centre st of the provisional sts. This will mark the beginning and end of all sleeve rounds. You should have ____(S) sts on your needle(s).

Size	32"	34"	36"	38"	40"	42"	44"	46"	48"	50"	52"	54"	56"	58"
S	79	82	87	91	98	104	111	117	122	129	135	138	144	149
T	40	9	8	10	4	7	56	9	11	9	8	12	0	10
U	0	5	9	18	7	13	0	10	20	8	15	23	0	13
V	39	8	7	9	3	6	55	8	11	8	7	11	144	9
W	80	96	96	96	112	112	112	128	128	144	144	144	144	160

Set-up Round 1: knit

Set-up Round 2: k ____(T) sts, m1b, *k____(U)[1] sts, m1b; rep from * to last ____(V) sts, k to end. [1](If U is 0, knit to end without increasing.)

You should now have ____(W) sts on your needle(s).

Round 1: *yo, skp, k11, k2tog, yo, k1; rep from * to end, sm.

Round 2 and all even-numbered rounds: knit

Round 3: *k1, yo, skp, k9, k2tog, yo, k2; rep from * to end, sm.

Round 5: *[yo, skp] x2, k7, [k2tog, yo] x2, k1; rep from * to end, sm.

Round 7: *k1, [yo, skp] x2, k5, [k2tog, yo] x2, k2; rep from * to end, sm.

Round 9: *[yo, skp] x3, k3, [k2tog, yo] x3, k1; rep from * to end, sm.

Round 11: *k1, [yo, skp] x3, k1, [k2tog, yo] x3, k2; rep from * to end, sm.

Round 13: *[yo, skp] x3, yo, sk2p, yo, [k2tog, yo] x3, k1; rep from * to end, sm.

Rounds 15 & 19: as Round 11.

Rounds 17 & 21: as Round 13.

Cast off (bind off) as for the skirt.

NECK EDGING

With the larger needle(s) pick up the provisional sts from the neckline. Cast on 3 sts before the first st, on the RS, then work an applied icord edging as follows: *k2, skp, return 3 sts to the passive needle; rep from * until all the provisional sts have been worked. Cast off the 3 icord sts.

FINISHING

Weave in all ends, then carefully block the cardigan. Soak it until thoroughly damp, then pin it out to the dimensions shown on the diagram on the next page. Take special care to pull out the points of the lace as shown. Apply buttons.

SKIRT LACE

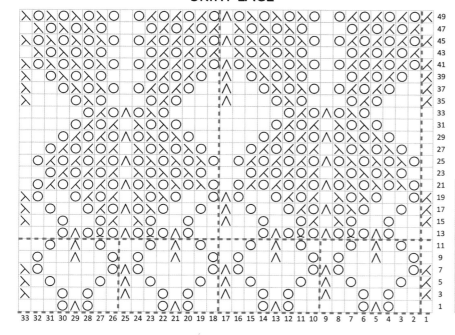

SKIRT LACE

RS rows: k6, follow chart, k6.

WS rows: k6, p to last 6 sts, k6.

Repeat rows 1–12 for a total of 48 rows (ie 4 times), then work rows 13–50.

St columns 2–9 form the pattern rep in rows 1–12.

St columns 2–17 form the pattern rep in Rows 13–50.

SLEEVE LACE

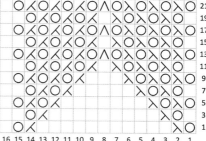

BLOCKING DIAGRAM

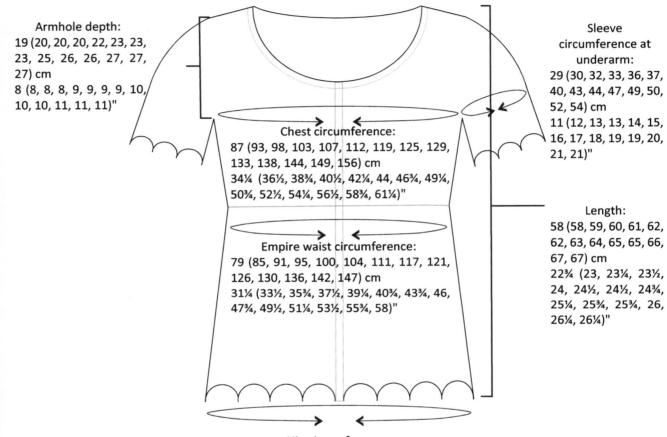

Neck edge circumference:
65 (68, 72, 72, 76, 78, 81, 83, 86, 86, 91, 95, 98, 101) cm
26 (27, 28, 28, 30, 31, 32, 33, 34, 34, 36, 37, 39, 40)"

Armhole depth:
19 (20, 20, 20, 22, 23, 23, 23, 25, 26, 26, 27, 27, 27) cm
8 (8, 8, 8, 9, 9, 9, 9, 10, 10, 10, 11, 11, 11)"

Sleeve circumference at underarm:
29 (30, 32, 33, 36, 37, 40, 43, 44, 47, 49, 50, 52, 54) cm
11 (12, 13, 13, 14, 15, 16, 17, 18, 19, 19, 20, 21, 21)"

Chest circumference:
87 (93, 98, 103, 107, 112, 119, 125, 129, 133, 138, 144, 149, 156) cm
34¼ (36½, 38¾, 40½, 42¼, 44, 46¾, 49¼, 50¾, 52½, 54¼, 56½, 58¾, 61¼)"

Length:
58 (58, 59, 60, 61, 62, 62, 63, 64, 65, 65, 66, 67, 67) cm
22¾ (23, 23¼, 23½, 24, 24½, 24½, 24¾, 25¼, 25¾, 25¾, 26, 26¼, 26¼)"

Empire waist circumference:
79 (85, 91, 95, 100, 104, 111, 117, 121, 126, 130, 136, 142, 147) cm
31¼ (33½, 35¾, 37½, 39¼, 40¾, 43¾, 46, 47¾, 49½, 51¼, 53½, 55¾, 58)"

Hip circumference:
98 (105, 112, 112, 119, 125, 132, 139, 145, 152, 152, 159, 166, 173) cm
38¾ (41¼, 44, 44, 46¾, 49¼, 52, 54¾, 57¼, 60, 60, 62¾, 65¼, 68)"

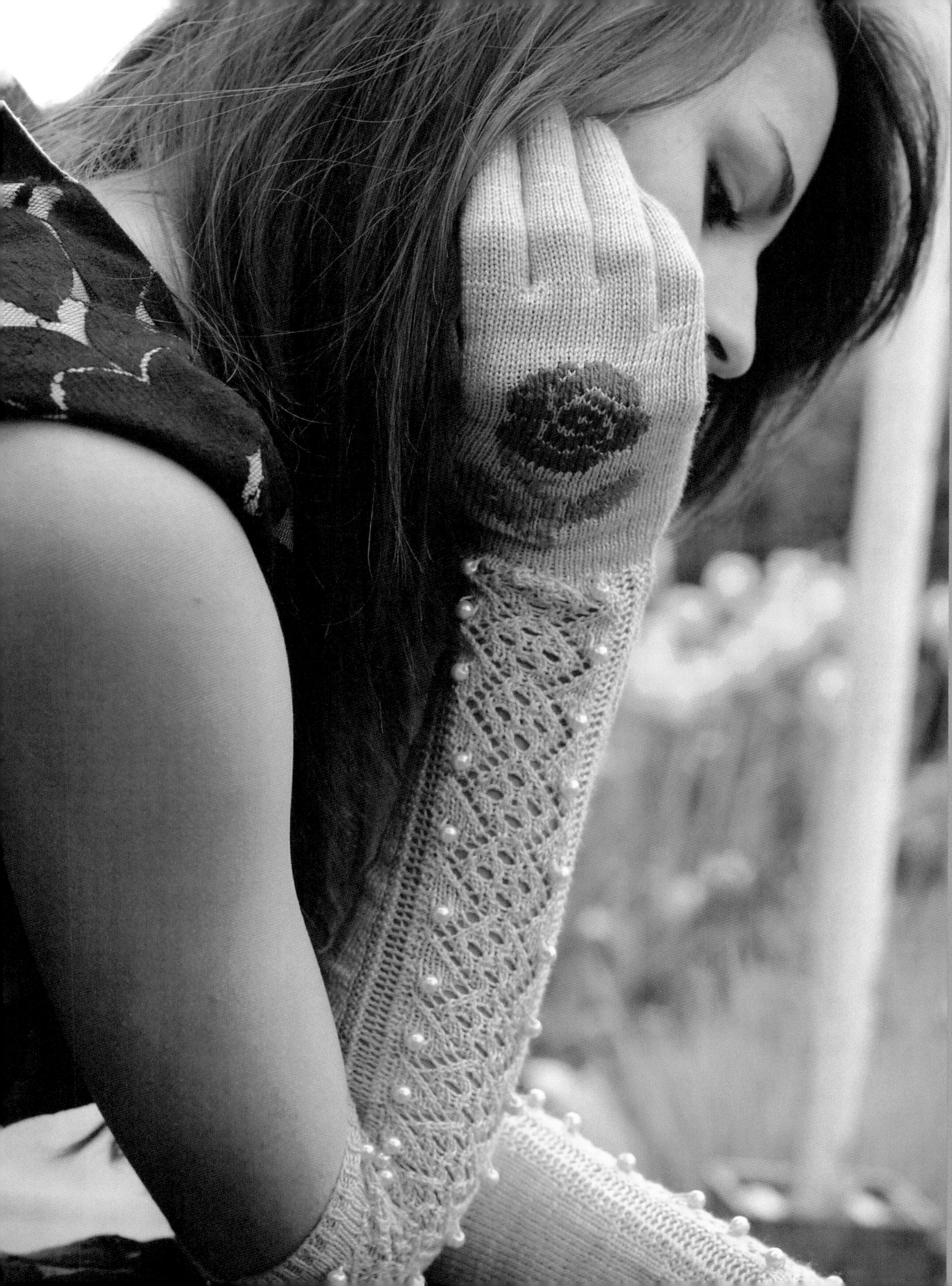

Prom

SIZE

Small:Medium:Large, for hand circumferences of 16½(19:21½)cm/6½(7½:8½)".

Finished measurements: approximately 62(64: 66)cm/24½(25¼:26)" long by 11½(12½:13½)cm/ 4¼:(4¾:5¼)" wide at the largest dimension.

MATERIALS

100g of 3ply/ light fingering weight silk or silk blend yarn in the main colour. Approximately 5 metres/5½ yards each of green and red silk embroidery threads.

52 medium-sized (6mm) beads.

The pictured sample was knitted in hand-dyed '100% Silk 4ply' (800m/874 yards per 100g) from The Knitting Goddess.

NEEDLES AND NOTIONS

2mm/US 0 needles (or size required to achieve the specified tension) for your preferred method of small diameter circular knitting; either 2 medium length circulars, 1 long circular (for magic loop method) or a set of DPNs. Darning/yarn needle. A pair of stitchmarkers.

TENSION

36 stitches and 48 rounds per 10cm/4" in stocking stitch/stockinette after blocking.

Instructions

SLEEVE

Thread 26 beads onto the yarn, then loosely cast on 78(87:96) stitches. Join for working in the round and work 5 rounds of single (k1, p1) rib.

Knit 7 rounds plain, then commence the lace pattern as follows:

Set-up round : k13, pm, k24, pm, k to end.

Round 1: k to marker, sm, k3, yo, k2tog, k1, pb, k3, yo, skp, k2tog, yo, k3, pb, k3, yo, k2tog, k1, sm, k to end.

Round 2: k to marker, sm, p1, p2tog, yo, p2, k14, p2tog, yo, p3, sm, k to end.

Round 3: k to marker, sm, k3, yo, k2tog, k3, k2tog, yo, k4, yo, skp, k5, yo, k2tog, k1, sm, k to end.

Round 4: As Round 2.

Round 5: k to marker, sm, k3, yo, k2tog, k2, k2tog, yo, k1, k2tog, yo twice, skp, k1, yo, skp, k4, yo, k2tog, k1, sm, k to end.

Round 6: k to marker, sm, p1, p2tog, yo, p2, k7, p1, k6, p2tog, yo, p3, sm, k to end.

Round 7: k to marker, sm, k3, yo, k2tog, k1, k2tog, yo, k8, yo, skp, k3, yo, k2tog, k1, sm, k to end.

Round 8: As Round 2.

Round 9: k to marker, sm, k3, yo, k2tog twice, yo, k1, k2tog, yo twice, skp, k2tog, yo twice, ssk, k1, yo, skp, k2, yo, k2tog, k1, sm, k to end.

Round 10: k to marker, sm, p1, p2tog, yo, p2, k5, p1, k3, p1, k4, p2tog, yo, p3, sm, k to end.

Round 11: k to marker, sm, k3, yo, k2tog, k2, yo, skp, k6, k2tog, yo, k4, yo, k2tog, k1, sm, k to end.

Round 12: As Round 2.

Round 13: k to marker, sm, k3, yo, k2tog, k3, yo, skp, k2tog, yo twice, skp, k2tog, yo, k5, yo, k2tog, k1, sm, k to end.

Round 14: As Round 6.

Round 15: k to marker, sm, k3, yo, k2tog, k4, yo, skp, k2, k2tog, yo, k6, yo, k2tog, k1, sm, k to end.

Round 16: k to 2 sts before marker, skp, sm, p1, p2tog, yo, p2, k14, p2tog, yo, p3, sm, k2tog, k to end.

Work the 16 round pattern 12 times in total. *54(63:72)sts*

Complete the sleeve and set up for the hand as follows:

Left glove:

k1, rm, k3, yo, k2tog, k1, yf, pb, s1, yb, k3, yo, ssk, k2tog, yo, k3, yf, pb, s1, yb, k3, yo, k2tog, k1, rm, k26(33:40), pm, k2, pm. You should have finished 1(3:5) sts before the end of the round.

Right glove:

k1, rm, k3, yo, k2tog, k1, yf, pb, s1, yb, k3, yo, ssk, k2tog, yo, k3, yf, pb, s1, yb, k3, yo, k2tog, k1, rm, k2(4:6), pm, k2, pm. You should have finished 25(32:39) sts before the end of the round.

HAND (instructions are the same for both gloves)

You will now work the hand in stocking stitch (stockinette). The last marker placed marks the new end/start of round.

Thumb gusset:

Rounds 1–3: knit, slipping all markers as you come to them.

Round 4: k to marker, sm, m1f, k to marker, m1b, sm.

Work rounds 1–4 a total of 8(9:10) times, then work rounds 1–3 one more time. *70(81:92)sts*

LACE PANEL

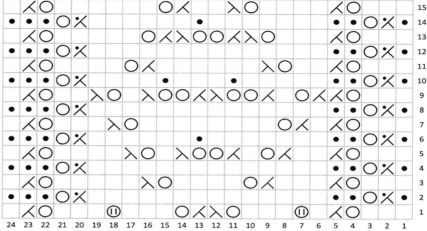

Refer to the written instructions for sleeve decreases before and after line 16 of the lace panel.

Divide for thumb:

Knit to marker, rm, place the next 16(18:20) sts (the gusset sts) onto waste yarn. Cast on 6 sts next to the last st worked, sm, then continue knitting around, starting with the first st after the reserved sts (ie the first st of the next round). There are now 60(69:78) sts in the round. Knit in st-st for 4(4½:5)cm/1½(1¾:2)" before dividing the round for the little finger.

Divide for little finger:

Knit 23(26:29) sts, place the next 14(17:20) sts (the little finger sts) onto waste yarn, then cast on 3 sts next to the last st worked. Continue knitting around, starting with the first st after the reserved sts. *49(55:61) sts*

Knit in st-st for 1½(2:2½)cm/½(¾:1)" before working the fingers as instructed on the next page.

Index finger:

Knit 9(10:11), place the next 31(35:39) sts (the hand sts) onto waste yarn, cast on 4 sts next to the last st worked, and then knit the last 9(10:11) sts of the round (ie the sts that follow the reserved sts). There should now be 22(24:26) sts in the round.

Knit until the finger measures 6½(7:7½)cm/ 2½(2¾:3)" from the 4 cast-on sts at the base.

Next round: [k2tog, k1] x7(8:8), k1(0:2). *15(16:18) sts*

Next 2 rounds: knit

Next round: k2tog x7(8:9), k1(0:0). *8(8:9) sts*

Break the yarn leaving a 15cm/6" tail. Thread this onto a darning needle and pull it through the remaining sts. Pull the yarn tight and then weave it through a few sts on the inside of the finger to secure the end.

Middle finger:

Joining in new yarn, pick up and knit the first 7(8:9) hand sts from the waste yarn. Then cast on 4 sts next to the last st worked. Leaving the next 17(19:21) hand sts on the waste yarn, transfer the last 7(8:9) hand sts from the waste yarn to your needles and knit them, working towards the first finger. Finally pick up and knit 4 sts from the base of the 4 that were cast on at the bottom of the first finger, ending where the yarn was joined in. There should now be 22(24:26) sts in the round.

Knit until the finger measures 7½(8:8½)cm/ 3(3¼:3½)" from the 4 cast-on sts at the base.

Next round: [k2tog, k1] x7(8:8), k1(0:2). *15(16:18) sts*

Next 2 rounds: knit

Next round: k2tog x7(8:9), k1(0:0). *8(8:9) sts*

Finish as for index finger.

Ring finger:

Joining in new yarn, pick up and knit the remaining 17(19:21) sts from the waste yarn. Then pick up and knit 4 sts from the base of the 4 that were cast on at the bottom of the second finger, ending where the yarn was joined in. There should now be 21(23:25) sts in the round.

Knit until the finger measures 6½(7:7½)cm/ 2½(2¾:3)" from the cast-on sts at the base.

Next round: [k2tog, k1] x7(7:8), k0(2:1). *14(16:17) sts*

Next 2 rounds: knit

Next round: k2tog x7(8:8), k0(0:1). *7(8:9) sts*

Finish as for index finger.

Little finger:

Joining in new yarn, pick up knit the 14(17:20) sts that were reserved for the little finger. Then pick up and knit 3 sts from the base of those cast on during the division of the round for the little finger. There should now be 17(20:23) sts in the round.

Knit until the finger measures 5½(6:6½)cm/ 2(2¼:2½)" from the 3 cast-on sts at the base.

Next round: [k2tog, k1] x5(6:7), k2. *12(14:16) sts*

Next 2 rounds: knit

Next round: k2tog x6(7:8). *6(7:8) sts*

Finish as for index finger.

Thumb:

Joining in new yarn, pick up and knit the 16(18:20) thumb gusset sts from the waste yarn. Then pick up and knit 6 sts from the base of those that were cast on above the thumb gusset. There should now be 22(24:26) sts in the round.

Knit until the thumb measures 6(6½:7)cm/ 2¼(2½:2¾)" from the 6 cast-on sts at the base.

Next round: [k2tog, k1] x7(8:8), k1(0:2). *15(16:18) sts*

Next 2 rounds: knit

Next round: k2tog x7(8:9), k1(0:0). *8(8:9) sts*

Finish as for index finger.

EMBROIDERY

Apply the rose motifs in duplicate stitch following the charts below. Take care to centre the motif on the back of the hand.

FINISHING

Weave in all ends inside the gloves.

The lace on the arms requires some stretching to accentuate the pattern. Stretch each arm over a shaped sleeve blocker cut from card. The blocker(s) should be 43cm/17" long, and should taper from 8(9:10)cm/3(3½:4)" wide to 11½(12½:13½)cm/4¼(4¾:5¼)" wide. Once on the blocker(s) press each glove under an ironing cloth with a warm steam iron, taking special care around the beads. Lightly press the hands also.

ROSE EMBROIDERY

Right hand

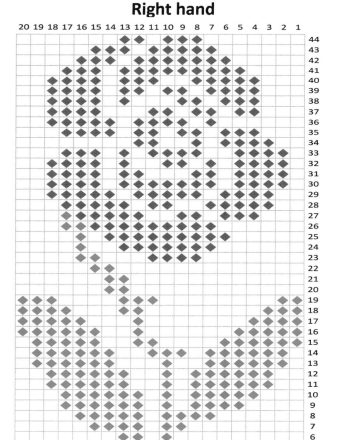

Left hand

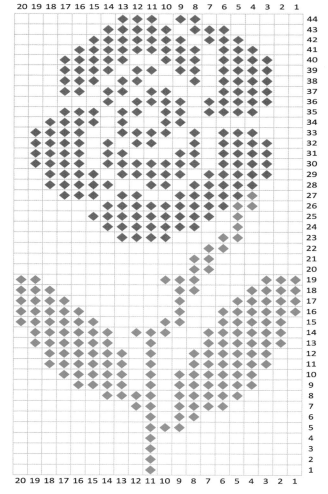

 35

SIZE

157cm/62" long and 51cm/20" wide.

MATERIALS

100g of 2ply laceweight wool and silk yarn with approximately 754 metres/825 yards per 100g.

The pictured sample was knitted with Alisha Goes Around 'Raft Of Otter Lace' (80% superwash blue faced leicester wool, 20% silk) in shade 'Figurine'.

NEEDLES

Three 120cm/47" 3.00mm/US 2½ circular needles.

Adjust needle size as necessary to achieve the specified tension.

TENSION/GAUGE

24 sts and 38 rounds per 10cm/4" in diamond lace pattern after blocking.

Instructions

CENTRAL LACE PANEL

Using Judy's 'magic' method, cast on 276 sts onto each of two needles. *(552 sts)*

Following either the charts, or the written instructions below, work 36 rounds of diamond lace pattern, changing needles for each half round:

Round 1: *[yo, k1] x2, pm, yo, k1, [yo, skp, k3, k2tog, yo, k1] x34, yo, k1, pm; rep from * for second half of round. *(560 sts)*

Round 2 and all even-numbered rounds: knit

Round 3: *yo, k3, yo, k1, sm, yo, k2, [k1, yo, skp, k1, k2tog, yo, k2] to 2 sts before next marker, k1, yo, k1, sm; rep from * for second half of round. *(568 sts)*

Round 5: *yo, k5, yo, k1, sm, yo, k3, [k2, yo, sk2p, yo, k3] to 3 sts before next marker, k2, yo, k1, sm; rep from * for second half of round. *(576 sts)*

Round 7: *yo, k7, yo, k1, sm, yo, k4, [k1, k2tog, yo, k1, yo, skp, k2] to 4 sts before next marker, k3, yo, k1, sm; rep from * for second half of round. *(584 sts)*

Round 9: *yo, k2, yo, skp, k1, k2tog, yo, k2, yo, k1, sm, yo, k2, yo, skp, k1, [k2tog, yo, k3, yo, skp, k1] to 5 sts before next marker, k2tog, yo, k2, yo, k1, sm; rep from * for second half of round. *(592 sts)*

Round 11: *yo, k4, yo, sk2p, yo, k4, yo, k1, sm, yo, k4, yo, sk2p, [yo, k5, yo, sk2p] to 5 sts before next marker, yo, k4, yo, k1, sm; rep from * for second half of round. *(600 sts)*

Round 13: *yo, k4, k2tog, yo, k1, yo, skp, k4, yo, k1, sm, yo, k4, k2tog, yo, k1, [yo, skp, k3, k2tog, yo, k1] to 7 sts before next marker, yo, skp, k4, yo, k1, sm; rep from * for second half of round. *(608 sts)*

Round 15: *yo, k1, yo, skp, k1, k2tog, yo, k3, yo, skp, k1, k2tog, yo, k1, yo, k1, sm, yo, [k1, yo, skp, k1, k2tog, yo, k2] to 8 sts before next marker, k1, yo, skp, k1, k2tog, yo, k1, yo, k1, sm; rep from * for second half of round. *(616 sts)*

Round 17: *yo, k1, [k2, yo sk2p, yo, k3] to 1 st before next marker, yo, k1, sm; rep from * to end. *(624 sts)*

Round 19: *yo, k2, [k1, k2tog, yo, k1, yo, skp, k2] to 2 sts before next marker, k1, yo, k1, sm; rep from * to end. *(632 sts)*

Round 21: *yo, k3, [k2tog, yo, k3, yo, skp, k1] to 3 sts before next marker, k2, yo, k1, sm; rep from * to end. *(640 sts)*

Round 23: *yo, k2, yo, sk2p, [yo, k5, yo, sk2p] to 3 sts before next marker, yo, k2, yo, k1, sm; rep from * to end. *(648 sts)*

Round 25: *yo, k2, k2tog, yo, k1, [yo, skp, k3, k2tog, yo, k1] to 5 sts before next marker, yo, skp, k2, yo, k1, sm; rep from * to end. *(656 sts)*

Round 27: *yo, k2, k2tog, yo, k2, [k1, yo, skp, k1, k2tog, yo, k2] to 6 sts before next marker, k1, yo, skp, k2, yo, k1; rep from * to end. *(664 sts)*

Round 29: *yo, k1, yo, sk2p, yo, k3, [k2, yo, sk2p, yo, k3] to 7 sts before next marker, k2, yo, sk2p, [yo, k1] x2, sm; rep from * to end. *(672 sts)*

Round 31: *yo, [k1, k2tog, yo, k1, yo, skp, k2] to 8 sts before next marker, k1, k2tog, yo, k1, yo, skp, k1, yo, k1, sm; rep from * to end. *(680 sts)*

Round 33: *yo, k1, [k2tog, yo, k3, yo, skp, k1] to 1 st before next marker, yo, k1, sm; rep from * to end. *(688 sts)*

Round 35: *yo, k1, k2tog, [yo, k5, yo, sk2p] to 9 sts before next marker, yo, k5, yo, skp, k1, yo, k1, sm; rep from * to end. *(696 sts)*

Round 36: knit

FEATHER AND FAN BORDER

Following either the charts, or the written instructions below, work 36 rounds of feather and fan lace pattern, changing needles for each half round:

Round 1: *yo, k2, [yo, k8] to 4 sts before marker, k3, yo, k1, sm; rep from * to end. *(788 sts)*

Round 2 and all even-numbered rounds: knit

Round 3: *yo, k1, k2tog, yo, **[k1, yo] x3, skp x3, k1, k2tog x3, [yo, k1] x2, yo,** rep from ** to ** to 5 sts before marker, k1, yo, skp, k1, yo, k1, sm; rep from * to end. *(796 sts)*

Rounds 5, 9, 13, 17, 21, 25, 29, and 33: *yo, knit to 1 st before marker, yo, k1, sm; rep from * to end.

Round 7: *yo, k2tog x2, yo, k1, yo, **[k1, yo] x3, skp x3, k1, k2tog x3, [yo, k1] x2, yo,** rep from ** to ** to 7 sts before marker, [k1, yo] x2, skp x2, yo, k1, sm; rep from * to end. *(812 sts)*

Round 11: *yo, k2, k2tog x2, yo, k1, yo, **[k1, yo] x3, skp x3, k1, k2tog x3, [yo, k1] x2, yo,** rep from ** to ** to 9 sts before marker, [k1, yo] x2, skp x2, k2, yo, k1, sm; rep from * to end. *(828 sts)*

Round 15: *yo, k1, k2tog x3, [yo, k1] x2, yo, **[k1, yo] x3, skp x3, k1, k2tog x3, [yo, k1] x2, yo,** rep from ** to ** to 11 sts before marker, [k1, yo] x3, skp x3, k1, yo, k1, sm; rep from * to end. *(844 sts)*

Round 19: *yo, k3, k2tog x3, [yo, k1] x2, yo, **[k1, yo] x3, skp x3, k1, k2tog x3, [yo, k1] x2, yo,** rep from ** to ** to 13 sts before marker, [k1, yo] x3, skp x3, k3, yo, k1, sm; rep from * to end. *(860 sts)*

Round 23: *yo, k2, yo, skp, k1, k2tog x3, [yo, k1] x2, yo, **[k1, yo] x3, skp x3, k1, k2tog x3, [yo, k1] x2, yo,** rep from ** to ** to 15 sts before marker, [k1, yo] x3, skp x3, k1, k2tog, yo, k2, yo, k1, sm; rep from * to end. *(876 sts)*

Round 27: *[yo, k1] x2, yo, skp x2, k1, k2tog x3, [yo, k1] x2, yo, **[k1, yo] x3, skp x3, k1, k2tog x3, [yo, k1] x2, yo,** rep from ** to ** to 17 sts before marker, [k1, yo] x3, skp x3, k1, k2tog x2, [yo, k1] x3, sm; rep from * to end. *(892 sts)*

Round 31: *yo, k2, [yo, k1] x2, skp x2, k1, k2tog, x3, [yo, k1] x2, yo, **[k1, yo] x3, skp x3, k1, k2tog x3, [yo, k1] x2, yo,** rep from ** to ** to 19 sts before marker, [k1, yo] x3, skp x3, k1, k2tog x2, [k1, yo] x2, k2, yo, k1, sm; rep from * to end. *(908 sts)*

Round 35: *yo, k1, **[k1, yo] x3, skp x3, k1, k2tog x3, [yo, k1] x2, yo,** rep from ** to ** to 3 sts before marker, k2, yo, k1, sm; rep from * to end. *(924 sts)*

Round 36: knit

GARTER STITCH EDGE

Work 6 rounds of garter stitch as follows:

Rounds 1, 3, and 5: *purl to 1 st before marker, yo, k1, sm; rep from * to end.

Rounds 2, 4, and 6: knit

Cast off (bind off): k1, *k1, return the 2 sts to passive needle, k2tog tbl; rep from * to end.

Break off the yarn leaving a short tail for weaving in.

FINISHING

Weave in all ends then block to the dimensions given on the diagram on the next page, taking care to pin out the lace points as shown.

Blocking diagram

51 cm/
20"

168 cm/66"

7½cm/ 3"

10cm/
4"

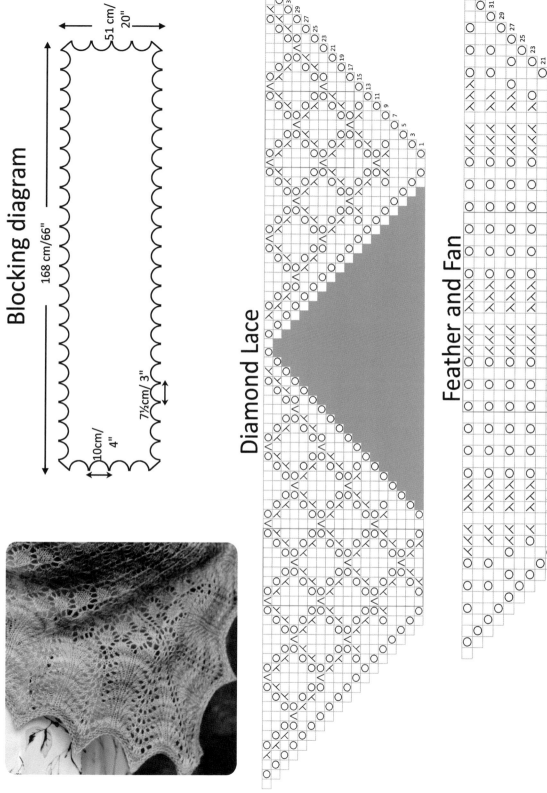

Diamond Lace

Feather and Fan

Red boxes outline
the pattern repeats.

Every leaf speaks bliss to me, fluttering from the autumn tree.
~Emily Bronte

A knitter friend bemoaned the unseasonable warm weather we were having one autumn. 'Why?' I asked, for I love warmth, and glory in an Indian summer. She answered 'It's meant to be cold, I want to walk through golden woods in my new jumper.' How knitters love to wear their handknits! So, I include here a warm paisley wrap, and a truly autumnal jumper featuring lacy golden leaf skeletons over a contrast underlayer.

We love to give handknits to others too. As autumn begins many knitters plan their 'Christmas knitting', a list of what project they will make for who. Small projects work well for long lists, so fingerless mittens are a great option for gift knitting if you have a large family.

Indian Summer

Mallorn

Sweetheart Mitts

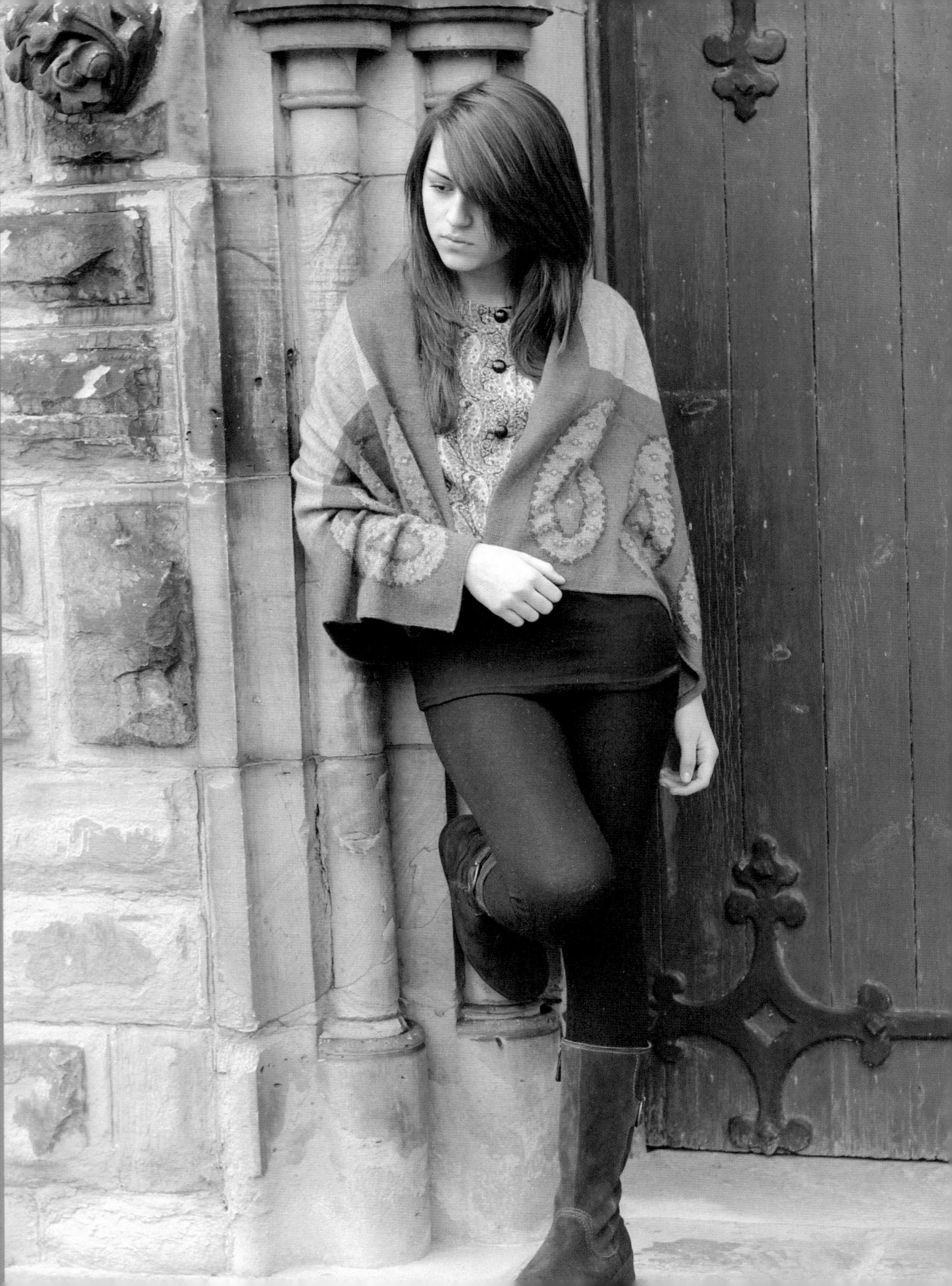

SIZE

140cm/55" long and 69cm/27" wide after blocking.

MATERIALS

Soft 2ply/laceweight yarn in natural fibres. The pictured sample was made with Louet Mooi. I recommend Malabrigo Lace as a widely available and budget-conscious alternative. You will require 5 colours in the following amounts (shades in parentheses are Malabrigo Lace):

A: Jade (Azul Profundo)–755 metres/825 yards

B: Aqua (Bobby Blue)–630 metres/690 yards

C: Spring Ruby (Damask Rose)–200 metres/220 yards

D: Espresso (Marron Oscuro)–100 metres/110 yards

E: Amber (Rhodesian)–45 metres/50 yards

NEEDLES

80cm/32" 2mm/US 0 circular needle and set of DPNs.

Adjust needle size as necessary to achieve the specified tension.

TENSION/GAUGE

40 sts and 48 rows per 10cm/4" in stocking stitch (stockinette) after blocking.

Instructions

FIRST BORDER

Cast on 3 sts in yarn A, then knit 256 rows of icord. Cast off (bind off), leaving the yarn attached.

Still working with yarn A, pick up and knit 256 sts along one edge of the icord.

Row 1 (WS): p to the last 3 sts, sl3 purlwise.

Row 2 (RS): k to the last 3 sts, sl3 purlwise.

Repeat these 2 rows until you have worked a total of 15 rows, ending with a WS row.

Commence the intarsia pattern in the next row as follows:

RS intarsia rows: k11 in yarn A, work across the relevant line of the paisley motif charts 4 times, k18 in yarn A, sl3 purlwise.

WS intarsia rows: p21 in yarn A, work across the relevant line of the paisley motif charts 4 times, p8 in yarn A, sl3 purlwise.

After completing all lines in the motif charts, work another 16 rows of st-st in yarn A, slipping the last 3 sts in each row purlwise. End with a WS row.

CENTRE

Row 1 (RS): k37 in yarn A, k182 in yarn B, k34 in yarn A, sl3 purlwise.

Row 2 (WS): p37 in yarn A, p182 in yarn B, p34 in yarn A, sl3 purlwise.

Repeat these 2 rows until the centre measures 75cm/29½", ending with a WS row.

SECOND BORDER

Work 16 rows of st-st in yarn A, slipping the last 3 sts in each row purlwise. End with a WS row.

Commence the intarsia pattern in the next row as follows, following the charts from the top down:

RS intarsia rows: k21 in yarn A, work across the relevant line of the paisley motif charts 4 times, k8 in yarn A, sl3 purlwise.

WS intarsia rows: p11 in yarn A, work across the relevant line of the paisley motif charts 4 times, p18 in yarn A, sl3 purlwise.

After completing all lines in the motif charts, work another 16 rows of st-st in yarn A, slipping the last 3 sts in each row purlwise. End with a WS row.

Work an applied icord cast-off (bind-off) as follows:

With the RS facing, cable cast on 3 sts next to the last st worked. Then *k2, skp, return 3 sts to the passive needle; rep from * until only the 3 icord sts remain. Cast off the icord sts.

FINISHING

Neatly tie off or weave in all ends on the wrong side of the intarsia. Weave in all other ends, then block the shawl to the stated dimensions.

Colour Key

■ Jade (Azul Profundo)

■ Espresso (Marron Oscuro)

□ Spring Ruby (Damask Rose)

□ Aqua (Bobby Blue)

■ Amber (Rhodesian)

INTARSIA TECHNIQUE TIPS

Work the intarsia motifs with small lengths of yarn (75cm/30"), using felted joins to add more yarn when required. This way tangles can be avoided; simply pull each yarn through when you need it.

Introducing new yarn lengths: leaving a short tail for tying or weaving in later, start knitting with the new yarn length.

RS colour changes: drop the yarn you have finished using, and bring the required yarn up behind it from below to knit it.

WS colour changes: drop the yarn you have finished using, and bring the required yarn up in front of it from below to purl it.

USING THE CHARTS

First border: Start at Stitch 1 of line 1. Follow RS rows from right to left, and WS rows from left to right. Make sure you only knit line 70 once—it is included in both Charts 1 and 2 to help with pattern placement.

Second border: Start at stitch 56 of line 140. Turn the charts upside down to follow them for this border. This way you will see the pattern oriented as it appears from the RS as you knit. With the charts upside down, follow RS rows from right to left, and WS rows from left to right, ie starting at the un-numbered end of all lines in the charts. Make sure you only knit line 70 once.

CHART 1

CHART 2

Indian Summer

SIZE

32(34:36:38:40:42:44:46:48:50:52:54:56:58)" chest.

MATERIALS

Heavy 4ply or sportweight wool and silk yarn with approximately 365 metres/400 yards per 100g. You will need 2(2:2:2:3:3:3:3:3:3:3:3:3:4) 100g skeins in MC and 1 100g skein in CC. You will also need 1 skein of 2ply/laceweight yarn in MC. As the MC is required in both sportweight and laceweight yarns, choose a brand that has the same colour range across different yarn weights.

The pictured sample was knitted with Fyberspates Scrumptious yarns in 'Gold' and 'Cherry' shades.

NEEDLES

3.5mm/US 4 needles needles for your preferred methods of small and large diameter circular knitting.

Adjust needle size as necessary to achieve the specified tensions.

TENSION/GAUGE

24 sts and 32 rounds per 10cm/4" in stocking stitch /stockinette and lace pattern after blocking.

24 rows per 4" in icord after blocking.

Take care to check your tension carefully before commencing, and adjust your needle sizes accordingly.

Instructions

DOUBLE YOKE

Using crochet provisional method cast on 3 sts in the CC yarn. Then knit ____(A) rows of icord as follows:

Icord row: k3, return all 3 sts to the passive needle.

Break off the yarn, leaving a 30cm/12" tail. Place the 3 icord sts onto a safety pin.

Working with the MC laceweight yarn, pick up ____(A) sts through the nearest side of the sts along one st column of the icord. Join for working in the round, then knit 22 rounds of lace pattern following the Yoke Chart or written instructions as follows:

Round 1: *k5, yo, sk2p, yo, k4; rep from * to end.

Round 2 and all even-numbered rounds: knit

Round 3: *k4, yo, skp, k1, k2tog, yo, k3; rep from * to end.

Round 5: *k3, lia, yo, skp, yo, sk2p, yo, k2tog, yo, lib, k2; rep from * to end.

Round 7: *k3, [yo, skp] x2, k1, [k2tog, yo] x2, k2; rep from * to end.

Round 9: *k2, [yo, skp] x2, yo, sk2p, yo, [k2tog, yo] x2, k1; rep from * to end.

Round 11: *k1, [yo, skp] x3, k1, [k2tog, yo] x3; rep from * to end.

Round 13: *k2, lia, [yo, skp] x2, yo, sk2p, yo, [k2tog, yo] x2, lib, k1; rep from * to end.

Round 15: *k4, [yo, skp] x2, k1, [k2tog, yo] x2, k3; rep from * to end.

Round 17: *k5, yo, skp, yo, sk2p, yo, k2tog, yo, k4; rep from * to end.

Round 19: *k6, yo, skp, k1, k2tog, yo, k5; rep from * to end.

Round 21: *k7, lia, yo, sk2p, yo, lib, k6; rep from * to end.

After completing Round 22 break off the yarn, leaving a short tail for weaving in. Leave the sts on a spare needle(s).

Size	32"	34"	36"	38"	40"	42"	44"	46"	48"	50"	52"	54"	56"	58"
A	132	144	144	156	156	168	168	168	168	180	180	192	192	204

Yoke Chart

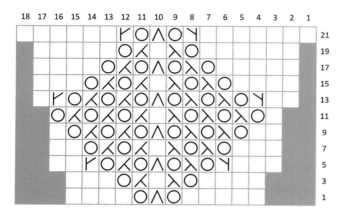

With the CC yarn pick up _____(A) sts through the icord. Pick up through the same st edges as for the laceweight sts, working behind the laceweight sts.

Knit 22 rounds with RS of lace facing you in front of the RS of the CC sts you are working on:

Rounds 1–4, 6–12, 14–20, and 22: knit

Round 5: *k3, lia, k7, lib, k2; rep from * to end.

Round 13: *k3, lia, k9, lib, k2; rep from * to end.

Round 21: *k3, lia, k11, lib, k2; rep from * to end.

Break off the yarn leaving a short tail for weaving in.

Now loosely work an icord cast-off (bind-off) with the CC and MC sts as follows:

Using crochet provisional method, cast on 3 sts in CC, placing the sts on the needle holding the laceweight sts. Hold this needle and the needle holding the CC yoke sts with the laceweight yoke sts RS facing you, and the CC yoke sts behind them (also with RS facing you). Commencing with the CC sts you have just cast on, continue as follows:

*K2, sl1 knitwise, knit together the next st from the front needle with the next st from the back needle, psso. Then return all 3 sts from the working needle to the front passive needle; rep from * until all the yoke sts have been worked.

Break off the yarn, leaving a 30cm/12" tail. Place the 3 icord sts onto a safety pin.

FRONT NECK AND SLEEVECAP SHAPING

Join in the MC sportweight yarn and pick up _____(B) sts from the icord cast-off. Pick up through the icord sts that are immediately next to the WS, CC sts from the upper yoke.

Increase round: k_____(C), [m1b, k_____(D)], _____(E) times, m1b, k_____(F).

You should now have _____(G) sts on your needle(s).

Size	32"	34"	36"	38"	40"	42"	44"	46"	48"	50"	52"	54"	56"	58"
B	198	216	216	234	234	252	252	252	252	270	270	288	288	306
C	8	18	9	30	13	63	21	10	13	19	11	24	12	39
D	14	36	18	58	16	126	42	21	15	33	19	48	24	76
E	13	5	11	3	13	1	5	11	15	7	13	5	11	3
F	8	18	9	30	13	63	21	11	14	20	12	24	12	39
G	212	222	228	238	248	254	258	264	268	278	284	294	300	310

Set up sleeve markers, and commence short row front neck shaping as follows:

Set-up Row 1 (RS): k____(H), pm, k____(I), pm, sl1 purlwise wyib, turn.

Set-up Row 2 (WS): sl1 purlwise wyib, sm, p to marker, sm, p____(J), pm, p____(I), pm, sl1 purlwise wyif, turn.

Shape sleevecap and continue short row neck shaping as follows:

Short Row 1 (RS): sl1 purlwise wyif, sm, m1f, k to marker, m1b, sm, k to marker, sm, m1f, k to marker, m1b, sm. Then knit together wrap with the st it wraps, sl1 purlwise wyib, turn.

Short Row 2 (WS): sl1 purlwise wyib, p1, [sm, p to marker] x3, sm. Then purl together wrap with the st it wraps, sl1 purlwise wyif, turn.

Short Row 3 (RS): sl1 purlwise wyif, [k to marker, sm, m1f, k to marker, m1b, sm] x2. Then knit to wrapped st, knit together wrap with the st it wraps, sl1 purlwise wyib, turn.

Short Row 4 (WS): sl1 purlwise wyib, [p to marker, sm] x4. Then purl to wrapped st, purl together wrap with the st it wraps, sl1 purlwise wyif, turn.

Work Short Rows 3 and 4 for a total of ____(K) rows.

Short Row 5 (RS): sl1 purlwise wyif, [k to 1 st before marker, m1b, k1, sm, m1f, k to marker, m1b, sm, k1, m1f] x2. Then knit to wrapped st, knit together wrap with the st it wraps, sl1 purlwise wyib, turn.

Short Row 6 (WS): as Short Row 4.

Work short rows 5 and 6 for a total of ____(L) rows.

Short Row 7 (RS): sl1 purlwise wyif, [k to marker, sm, m1f, k to marker, m1b, sm] x2. Then knit to wrapped st, knit together wrap with the st it wraps, k1, sl1 purlwise wyib, turn.

Short Row 8 (WS): sl1 purlwise wyib, [p to marker, sm] x4. Then purl to wrapped st, purl together wrap with the st it wraps, p1, sl1 purlwise wyif, turn.

Work Short Rows 7 and 8 for a total of ____(M) rows.

Short Row 9 (RS): sl1 purlwise wyif, [k to 1 st before marker, m1b, k1, sm, m1f, k to marker, m1b, sm, k1, m1f] x2. Then knit to wrapped st, knit together wrap with the st it wraps, k1, sl1 purlwise wyib, turn.

Short Row 10 (WS): as Short Row 8.

Work Short Rows 9 and 10 for a total of ____(N) rows.

Size	32"	34"	36"	38"	40"	42"	44"	46"	48"	50"	52"	54"	56"	58"
H	42	43	45	46	48	49	49	51	51	52	54	55	57	58
I	22	24	24	26	28	28	30	30	32	34	34	36	36	38
J	84	87	90	93	96	99	99	102	102	105	108	111	114	117
K	22	24	24	26	26	24	22	20	18	18	16	16	14	14
L	0	0	0	0	0	2	6	8	12	12	14	16	18	20
M	6	4	2	0	0	0	0	0	0	0	0	0	0	0
N	8	10	12	14	16	16	16	16	16	18	18	18	18	18

BODY

Return to working in the round, removing the sleeve sts and casting on underarm sts as follows:

Set-up round 1: sl1 purlwise wyib, [k to marker, rm. Place all sts before next marker onto waste yarn for sleeve. Then, continuing immediately next to the last st worked, cast on ____(O) sts using crochet provisional method, rm] x2. [Knit to wrapped st, knit together wrap with the st it wraps] x2. Knit to centre point of the first underarm sts, pm for end of round.

You should now have ____(P) sts on your needle(s).

Set-up round 2: k to centre point of the next underarm sts, pm, k to marker, sm.

Now knit 16 rounds in st-st, slipping each marker as you come to it.

Decrease as follows in the next, and every following 6th round until you have worked 9 decrease rounds in total.

Decrease round: [k1, skp, k to 3 sts before marker, k2tog, k1, sm] x2.

You should now have ____(Q) sts on your needle(s).

Now knit 12 rounds in st-st, slipping each marker as you come to it. You may adjust waist and overall length to fit by adding or removing rounds at this point.

Then increase as follows in the next, and every following 3rd round until you have worked ____(R) increase rounds in total.

Increase round: [k2, m1f, k to 2 sts before marker, m1b, k2, sm] x2.

You should now have ____(S) sts on your needle(s).

Now work 24 rounds in k4, p2 rib as follows, slipping the markers as you come to them:

Rib round: k2, *p2, k4; rep from * to last 4 sts, p2, k2.

Cast off (bind off) loosely in rib.

SLEEVES *(both alike)*

Place removed sts for one sleeve onto your needle(s). Pick up and knit ____(O) underarm provisional sts. Then knit the sleeve sts. Join for working in the round and knit to the centre point of the underarm provisional sts. Place marker for end of round.

You should now have ____(T) sts on your needle(s).

Size	32"	34"	36"	38"	40"	42"	44"	46"	48"	50"	52"	54"	56"	58"
O	4	6	6	8	8	10	12	12	14	16	16	18	18	20
P	192	206	216	230	240	254	266	276	288	302	312	326	336	350
Q	156	170	180	194	204	218	230	240	252	266	276	290	300	314
R	9	10	9	10	9	10	10	9	9	10	9	10	9	10
S	192	210	216	234	240	258	270	276	288	306	312	330	336	354
T	64	70	70	76	80	82	88	88	94	100	100	106	106	112

Knit 25 rounds in st-st, slipping the marker as you come to it. You may adjust sleeve length to fit by adding or removing rounds at this point.

Then decrease as follows in the next, and every following _____(U) round until you have worked _____(V) decrease rounds in total.

Decrease round: k1, skp, k to 3 sts before marker, k2tog, k1, sm.

You should now have _____(W) sts on your needle(s).

Knit _____(X) rounds in st-st. You may also adjust sleeve length to fit by adding or removing rounds at this point.

Now work 16 rounds in k4, p2 rib as follows, slipping the marker as you come to it:

Rib round: k2, *p2, k4; rep from * to last 4 sts, p2, k2.

Cast off (bind off) loosely in rib.

FINISHING

Neatly graft the reserved icord sts to the icord cast-on edges. Weave in all ends, then block to the dimensions shown in the diagram on the next page.

Size	32"	34"	36"	38"	40"	42"	44"	46"	48"	50"	52"	54"	56"	58"
U	9th	7th	9th	7th	6th	6th	5th	6th	5th	4th	4th	3rd	3rd	3rd
V	11	14	11	14	16	17	20	17	20	23	23	26	26	29
W	42	42	48	48	48	48	48	54	54	54	54	54	54	54
X	12	11	12	11	12	6	7	6	7	14	14	27	27	18

BLOCKING DIAGRAM

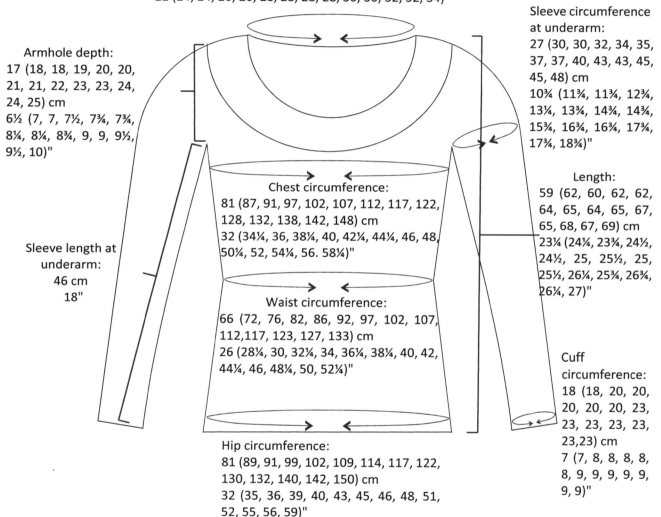

Neck edge circumference:
56 (61, 61, 66, 66, 71, 71, 71, 71, 76, 76, 81, 81, 86) cm
22 (24, 24, 26, 26, 28, 28, 28, 28, 30, 30, 32, 32, 34)"

Sleeve circumference
at underarm:
27 (30, 30, 32, 34, 35,
37, 37, 40, 43, 43, 45,
45, 48) cm
10¾ (11¾, 11¾, 12¾,
13¼, 13¾, 14¾, 14¾,
15¾, 16¾, 16¾, 17¾,
17¾, 18¾)"

Armhole depth:
17 (18, 18, 19, 20, 20,
21, 21, 22, 23, 23, 24,
24, 25) cm
6½ (7, 7, 7½, 7¾, 7¾,
8¼, 8¼, 8¾, 9, 9, 9½,
9½, 10)"

Length:
59 (62, 60, 62, 62,
64, 65, 64, 65, 67,
65, 68, 67, 69) cm
23¼ (24¼, 23¾, 24½,
24½, 25, 25½, 25,
25½, 26¼, 25¾, 26¾,
26¼, 27)"

Chest circumference:
81 (87, 91, 97, 102, 107, 112, 117, 122,
128, 132, 138, 142, 148) cm
32 (34¼, 36, 38¼, 40, 42¼, 44¼, 46, 48,
50¼, 52, 54¼, 56. 58¼)"

Sleeve length at
underarm:
46 cm
18"

Waist circumference:
66 (72, 76, 82, 86, 92, 97, 102, 107,
112,117, 123, 127, 133) cm
26 (28¼, 30, 32¼, 34, 36¼, 38¼, 40, 42,
44¼, 46, 48¼, 50, 52¼)"

Cuff
circumference:
18 (18, 20, 20,
20, 20, 20, 23,
23, 23, 23, 23,
23,23) cm
7 (7, 8, 8, 8, 8,
8, 9, 9, 9, 9, 9,
9, 9)"

Hip circumference:
81 (89, 91, 99, 102, 109, 114, 117, 122,
130, 132, 140, 142, 150) cm
32 (35, 36, 39, 40, 43, 45, 46, 48, 51,
52, 55, 56, 59)"

SIZE

Small:Medium:Large, for hand circumferences of 16½:19:21½ cm (6½:7½:8½"). If between sizes make the smaller size.

Finished measurements: 8¼:9½:10¾cm (3¼:3¾:4¼") wide by 21½ cm (8½") long from the top of the glove to the end of the lace points in the cuff.

MATERIALS

Approximately 50g each (200 metres/220 yards each) of any even 4ply/fingering weight yarn in two shades. The pictured sample used hand-dyed 'Merino Sock 100%' from The Yarn Yard in 'Rice Bowl', and 'Peach'.

NEEDLES AND NOTIONS

2.25mm/US 1 and 2.75mm/US 2 needles (or size required to achieve the specified tension) for your preferred method of small diameter circular knitting; either 2 medium length circulars, 1 long circular (for magic loop method) or a set of DPNs. Darning/yarn needle.

TENSION/GAUGE

After blocking 36 sts and 38 rounds per 10cm/4" in stranded pattern knitted on the larger needles.

Instructions

MAIN HAND

With the larger needle use a provisional method (eg crochet provisional) to cast on 60(68:76) sts in CC. Join for working in the round and knit 1 round in CC.

Leaving CC attached, join in MC and knit 1 round in MC.

Now commence the stranded pattern, starting with line 1 of Chart A (Main Hand). Work across the chart twice in each round, knitting the sts for your size as indicated in the chart key.

After completing 8 rounds of the charted pattern commence the thumb gusset..

THUMB GUSSET

In all rounds work across Chart A once, commencing with line 9. Then knit the first 1(3:3) sts of Chart A. Then knit across Chart B (Thumb Gusset), commencing with line 1. Then knit across Chart A again, commencing from st column 11(9:9).

Work the charted increases in MC.

Lines 1–16 of Chart A form a pattern repeat. So, after the round in which you follow line 16 of Chart A, return to line 1.

After completing line 28 of the thumb gusset, remove the gusset sts and cast on new sts in the next round as follows:

Knit once across line 5 of Chart A. Then knit the first 1(3:3) sts of Chart A. Remove the next 21 sts (the thumb gusset sts) and place them onto waste yarn. Then use a provisional method to cast on 5 sts in the working MC yarn. Take care to cast on the sts so that they sit snugly next to the sts you have just knitted. Finally, knit across Chart A again, commencing from st column 11(9:9), and keeping the tension tight for the first few sts. *60(68:76) sts*

TOP HAND

Continue in pattern from line 6 of Chart A. Stop when you have completed 3½ repeats of the Chart A pattern in the main hand, ending with a line 9 of pattern.

Leaving both yarns attached, knit a round in MC. Then break off MC, leaving a short tail for weaving in later.

Working in CC with the smaller needle, knit 1 round plain, then work 5 rounds of k1, p1 rib.

Cast off using the tubular cast-off/bind-off method as follows:

Round 1: *sl1 knitwise wyib, p1; repeat from * to end.

Round 2: *k1, sl1 purlwise wyif; repeat from * to end.

Divide the sts from the round onto separate needles so that all the knits are on 1 needle/set of needles, and all the purls are on a different needle/set of needles.

Break off the yarn leaving a 60cm/24" tail. Thread this onto a darning/yarn needle. Holding the purl sts behind the knits, graft the 2 sets of sts together using kitchener stitch. Maintain a loose tension throughout.

LACE CUFF

Place the sts from the first provisional cast-on onto your larger needle(s). If necessary pick up an extra st to make 60(68:76) sts. Join in MC and work a set-up round as follows, following the instructions for your chosen size:

Small size: knit

Medium size: k9, m1f, [k17, m1f] x3, k8. *(72 sts)*

Large size: k5, m1f, [k10, m1f, k9, m1f] x3, k10, m1f, k4. *(84 sts)*

Now follow either Chart C (Lace Cuff) or the written instructions below to knit the lace pattern for the cuff, working all alternate rounds (even-numbered rounds) in plain knit.

Round 1: *k10, k2tog, yo; repeat from * to end.

Round 2 and all even-numbered rounds: knit.

Round 3: *skp, k7, k2tog, yo, k1, yo; repeat from * to end.

Round 5: *skp, k5, k2tog, yo, k3, yo; repeat from * to end.

Round 7: *skp, k3, [k2tog, yo] x2, k1, yo, skp, yo; repeat from * to end.

Round 9: *skp, k1, [k2tog, yo] x2, k3, yo skp, yo; repeat from * to end.

Round 11: *sk2p, [yo, k2tog] x2, yo, k1, [yo, skp] x2, yo; repeat from * to end.

After working Round 11 break off the MC yarn. Leaving a short tail for weaving in later. Join in the CC yarn and cast (bind) off loosely as follows:

1 st at a time, sl2 knitwise to the working (right-hand) needle, *then return both sts from the working to the passive needle (with reversed mount) and knit them together tbl, sl the next st knitwise; repeat from * until all sts have been cast off, including the last yo of Round 11. Break off the yarn leaving a 15cm/6"tail. Thread this onto a darning/yarn needle and pull it through the remaining st, then take it under the first st from the cast-off, then back into the last st from the cast-off.

THUMB

Place the 21 sts from the waste yarn and 6 provisional sts from above the thumbhole onto the smaller needle(s). *(27 sts)*

Join in the CC yarn and continue as follows:

Round 1: k to the last 2 sts, k2tog. *(26 sts)*

Rounds 2-6: k1, p1; repeat from * to end.

Work a tubular cast-off (bind-off), following the instructions given for casting off the top of the hand.

FINISHING

Weave in all ends on the inside of the mitt, then block the mitt to the dimensions given on page 55, Soak and pin out the gloves to shape until thoroughly dry, Take extra care to evenly pull out and pin the points of the lace cuff.

Repeat all instructions to make the 2nd mitt.

CHART A–MAIN HAND

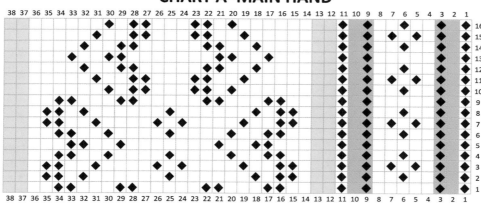

CHART B–THUMB GUSSET

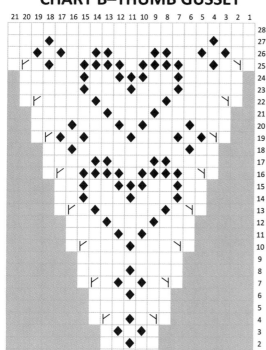

medium and large sizes only

large size only

CHART C–LACE CUFF

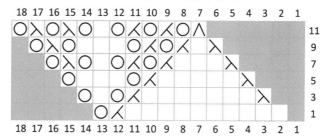

Winter is the time for comfort, for good food and warmth, for the touch of a friendly hand and for a talk beside the fire: it is the time for home.
~Edith Sitwell

In England winter always seems to be very, very long! Thankfully Christmas provides plenty of warmth for the heart with the joy of giving. Small projects in thick yarn make great last-minute gift knits. The Avé slippers even have a festive theme!

Of course, knitters need not fear the cold of winter. We can wrap ourselves in snuggly handknits made from super-warm fibres. The coat featured here is made from a blend of alpaca and wool, designed to keep you cosy on the coldest of days.

As well as knitting for warmth, knitters love to knit for fun. So I also include a sweet little stuffed heart ornament to bedeck your tree.

Adore

Anwen

Avé

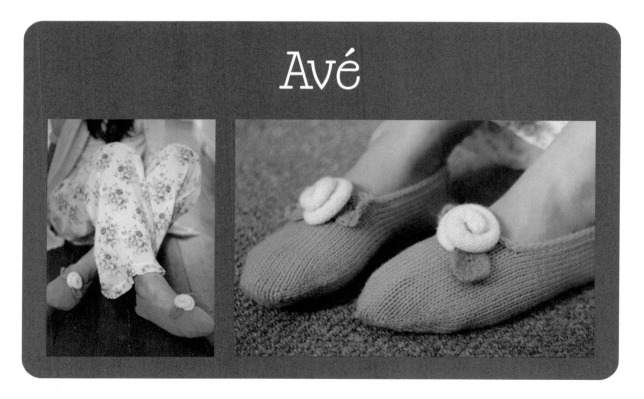

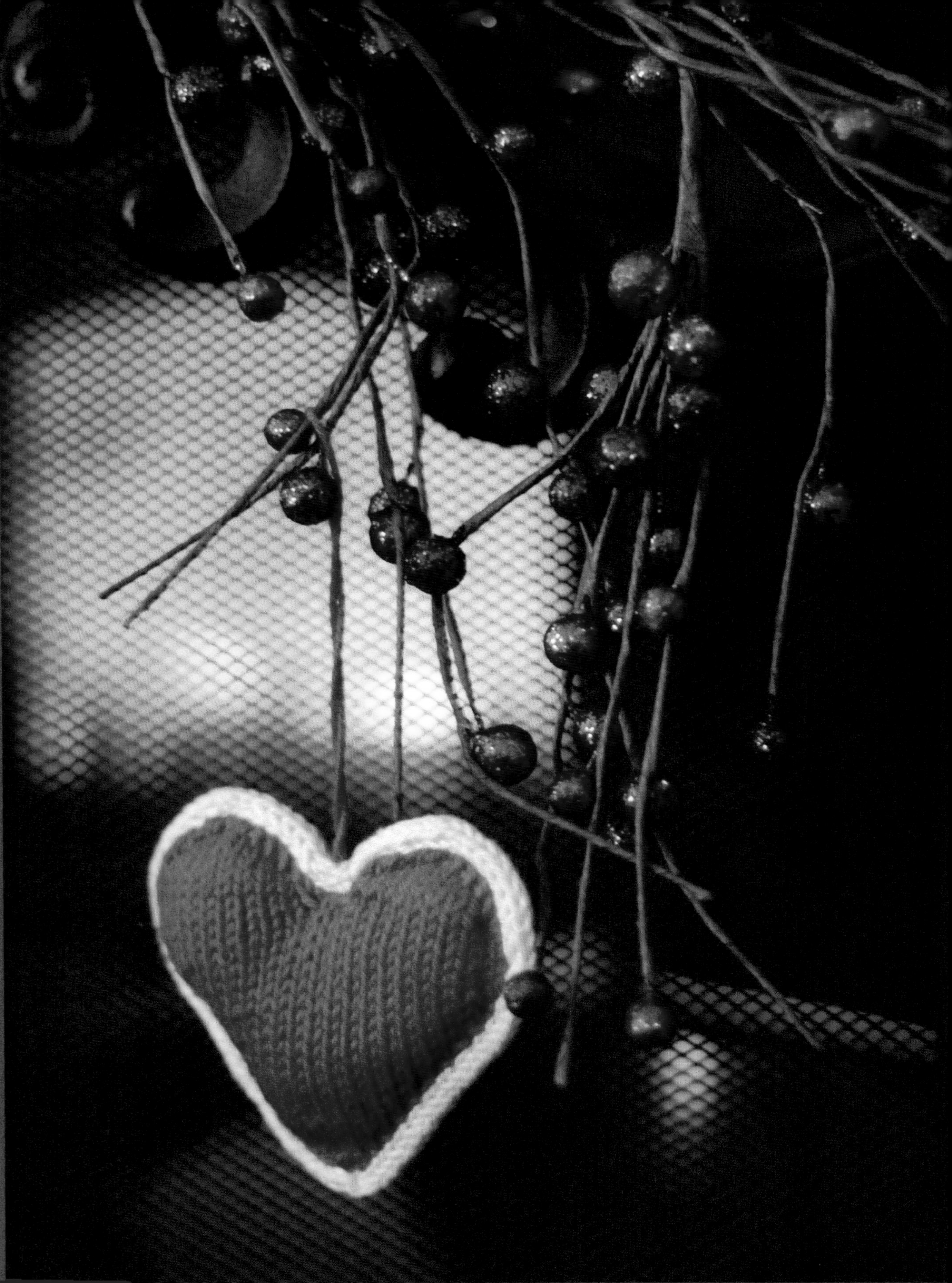

SIZE

Approximately 9cm/3½" wide and 8cm/3" high. Larger/smaller sizes may be made with different yarn and at a different tension/gauge to that specified below. Yarn quantities given below are for a heart knitted at the given tension/gauge.

MATERIALS

Any light DK/sportweight yarn in two colours. Approximately 15 metres/16½ yards of main colour, and 5½ metres/6 yards of contrast colour. The pictured samples used 'Patons 100% Cotton' DK in 'Red' and 'Cream'.

A small quantity of wool or polyester fibre for stuffing. You may like to scent the stuffing with essential oils or dried lavender.

TOOLS

3.25mm/US 3 needles (or size required to achieve the specified tension) for your preferred method of small diameter circular knitting; either two medium length circulars, one long circular (for magic loop method) or a set of DPNs. Darning/yarn needle.

TENSION/GAUGE

28 sts and 40 rounds per 10cm/4" in stocking stitch/stockinette knitted in the round.

YARN MANAGEMENT

In every round when you reach the CC sts drop the MC yarn. Pick up the CC and carry it tightly across the back of the CC sts. Tightly knit the CC sts. Then drop the CC and pick up the MC again. Maintaining a tight tension carry the MC yarn across the back of the CC sts, carrying it over the dropped CC yarn. Continue with the round leaving the CC where it is until you reach the CC sts again in the next round.

Instructions

The heart is knitted from the bottom point upwards.

Before starting divide the CC yarn into four lengths: 2 pieces measuring 1.8 metres/2 yards each, and 2 pieces measuring 0.9 metres/1 yard each.

For the cast-on you will need the MC yarn, and the two longer pieces of CC yarn.

MAIN HEART

Holding the tail end of the MC yarn as the thumb yarn throughout, use long-tail cast-on method to cast on 10 sts as follows. MC forms the base of all 10 sts, both MC and CC sts. Use the two longer pieces of CC yarn for the CC sts; one piece for each 3-st set. Leave a short 15cm/6" tail of the CC yarn at the beginning of each 3-st set.

*Cast on 2 sts in MC, then 3 sts in CC, repeat from * once. *(10 sts)*

Carefully join for working in the round and continue as follows:

Round 1: [k2 in MC, k3 in CC] x2.

Round 2: [In MC: k1, lia, lib, k1. In CC: k3] x2. *(14 sts)*

Round 3: [k in MC to CC piping, k3 in CC] x2.

Round 4: [In MC: k1, lia, k to 1 st before CC piping, lib, k1. In CC: k3] x2.

Repeat Rounds 3 and 4 until you have increased the total st count to 50 sts (22 MC sts on each side of the heart, plus the CC piping sts).

Repeat Round 3 another 3 times.

Leave all yarns attached.

Before commencing the first arch, neatly weave in the MC tail yarn at the bottom point of the heart.

Then use the CC tails to neatly graft the bottom of the pipings together, covering the MC base of each piping as you do so. Weave in the CC tails.

FIRST ARCH

Set-up round: k11 in MC, then place the next 25 sts onto waste yarn. Continuing immediately next to the last MC st you knitted, cast on 3 sts in CC with one of the shorter pieces of yarn. Continuing immediately next to the new CC sts, k11 in MC, then k3 in CC.

Rounds 1–3: [k11 in MC, k3 in CC] x2.

Rounds 4–7: [In MC: k2tog, k to 2 sts before the CC piping, skp. In CC: k3] x2.

12 sts remain; 6 MC sts and 6 CC sts.

Join the top of the heart as follows:

Return the 3 CC sts just knitted to the passive needle and knit them again in CC. Then place these 3 sts onto waste yarn or a safety pin.

Now break off the MC yarn leaving a 15cm/6" tail. Thread this onto the darning needle. Using kitchener st graft together the MC sts from the front and the back of the arch. Weave in the end.

In CC knit the remaining CC from the passive needle. Then return the other CC piping sts to a/the spare needle. Thread one of the CC yarn ends onto the darning needle. Using kitchener st graft together the two sets of CC piping sts.

Catch-stitch each CC yarn end under the centre st of the MC graft. Neatly weave in both CC yarn ends.

SECOND ARCH

Weave in the CC tail at the bottom of the short centre piping in the first arch.

Now place the sts from the waste yarn onto your needles. Then cast on 3 sts at the centre of the heart with the remaining short length of CC yarn. Leaving a 20cm/8" tail, join in the MC. Continue from the centre of the heart as for the first arch, commencing with Rounds 1–3.

Leave the CC tail at the bottom of the short centre piping in this second arch.

FINISHING

There is a small opening at the centre of the heart, where you joined in the MC. Stuff the heart through this opening.

After stuffing the heart, thread the remaining CC tail onto the darning needle. Use it to neatly join the bottom of the two centre pipings, then weave in the end.

Next thread the MC yarn onto the darning needle. Use this to close the holes at the centre on each side of the heart. If you are making a hanging ornament also use it to make a hanging loop above the centre of the heart. Finally, weave in the end.

Cherish!

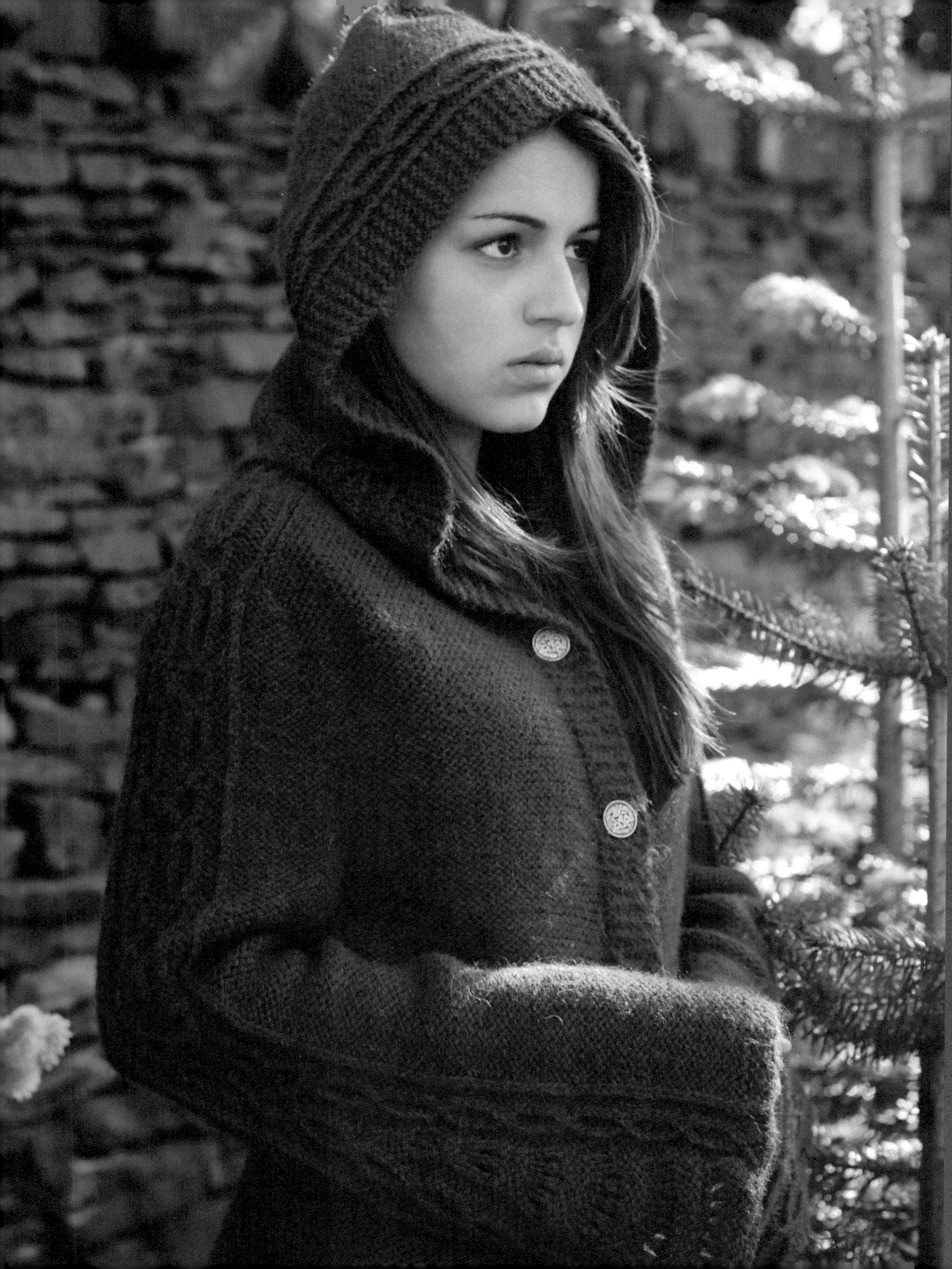

SIZE

To fit 32(34:36:38:40:42:44:46:48:50:52:54:56:58)" chests. The finished coat has 3–4" of positive ease.

MATERIALS

Aran/heavy worsted wool and alpaca yarn with approximately 132 metres/144 yards per 100g. You will need 14(15:15:16:17:17:18:18:19:19:20:21: 21:22) 100g skeins.

The pictured sample was knitted with Artesano Aran in the 'Nightfall' shade.

NEEDLES AND NOTIONS

5mm/US 8 needles for small diameter circular knitting, and a 5mm/US 8 120cm/47" circular needle.

Adjust needle size as necessary to achieve the specified tensions.

Six stitchmarkers. Seven 20mm/¾" buttons.

TENSION/GAUGE

17 sts and 21 rows per 10cm/4" in reverse st-st after blocking.

7cm/2¾" across main 16-st cable panel.

Instructions

NECK AND SHOULDERS

With the long circular needle, cast on 3 sts and knit ____(A) rows of icord as follows:

Icord row: k3, return all 3 sts to the passive needle.

Cast off the icord sts, leaving the final st from the cast-off on your needle. Then pick up and knit ____(A) sts through the nearest side of the sts along one st column of the icord, passing the final cast-off st over the first st as you go.

Set-up row (WS): k____(B), **pm, [p1tbl, k2] x5, p1tbl, pm**, k____(C), repeat from ** to **, k to end.

Set-up Row 2 (RS): k7 [p to 1 st before marker, m1bp, p1, sm, work across chart for 'Main Cable Panel', sm, p1, m1fp] x2, sl1 purlwise wyib, turn.

Set-up Row 3 (WS): sl1 purlwise wyib, [k to 1 st before marker, m1f, k1, sm, work across chart for 'Main Cable Panel', sm, k1, m1b] x2, k1, sl1 purlwise wyif, turn.

Short Row 1 (RS): sl1 wyif [p to 1 st before marker, m1bp, p1, sm, work across chart for 'Main Cable Panel', sm, p1, m1fp] x2, p to wrapped st of previous row, sl1 purlwise, from below lift the wrap onto the passive needle, return slipped st to passive needle, p together the st and wrap, s1 purlwise wyib, turn.

Short Row 2: (WS): sl1 purlwise wyib, [k to 1 st before marker, m1f, k1, sm, work across chart for 'Main Cable Panel', sm, k1, m1b] x2, k to wrapped st of previous row, from above lift the back of the wrap onto the passive needle, knit together the wrap and the st, sl1 purlwise wyif, turn.

Work Short Rows 1 and 2 for a total of 8 rows.

Final RS Short Row: sl1 wyif [p to 1 st before marker, m1bp, p1, sm, work across chart for 'Main Cable Panel', sm, p1, m1fp] x2, k to wrapped st of previous row, sl1 purlwise, from below lift the wrap onto the passive needle, return slipped st to passive needle, p together the st and wrap, p to last 7 sts, k7.

Size	32"	34"	36"	38"	40"	42"	44"	46"	48"	50"	52"	54"	56"	58"
A	72	80	86	88	94	96	96	98	102	104	110	112	120	122
B	12	14	16	16	18	18	18	18	20	20	22	22	24	24
C	16	20	22	24	26	28	28	30	30	32	34	36	40	42

MAIN CABLE PANEL

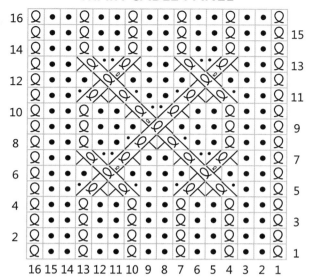

Final WS Short Row: [k to 1 st before marker, m1f, k1, sm, work across chart for 'Main Cable Panel', sm, k1, m1b] x2, k to wrapped st of previous row, from above lift the back of the wrap onto the passive needle, knit together the wrap and the st, k to end.

Place a 'one-row buttonhole' at the end of the next row (see next page) then every following ____(D) rows, counting the empire line icord as 2 rows, until you have worked 7 buttonholes in total.

Repeat the following 2 rows for a total of 12 rows, ending with a WS row.

RS Shoulder Row: k7 [p to 1 st before marker, m1bp, p1, sm, work across chart for 'Main Cable Panel', sm, p1, m1fp] x2, p to last 7 sts k7.

WS Shoulder Row: [k to 1 st before marker, m1f, k1, sm, work across chart for 'Main Cable Panel', sm, k1, m1b] x2, k to end.

You should now have ____(E) sts on your needle.

SLEEVECAP SHAPING

Set-up Row (RS): k7, [p to marker, sm, m1fp, work across chart for 'Main Cable Panel', m1bp, sm] x2, p to last 7 sts, k7.

Work sleevecap increases in the next ____(F) rows as follows, maintaining the cable panels, reverse st-st, and button bands as set. (Last row is a WS row.)

WS increase rows: work an m1b immediately after the 1st and 3rd markers. Work an m1f immediately before the 2nd and 4th markers.

RS increase rows: work an m1fp immediately after the 1st and 3rd markers. Work an m1bp immediately before the 2nd and 4th markers.

Then increase in every following 4th row until you have worked the increase row ____(G) times more. Work all other rows without increasing.

Then increase in every row for a total of ____(H) rows, working the RS rows as above and the WS rows as follows:

WS increase rows: work an m1bp 1 st before the 1st and 3rd markers. Work an m1fp 1 st after the 2nd and 4th markers.

You should now have ____(I) sts in total.

Size	32"	34"	36"	38"	40"	42"	44"	46"	48"	50"	52"	54"	56"	58"
D	22	24	24	24	26	26	26	26	28	28	28	28	30	30
E	168	176	182	184	190	192	192	194	198	200	206	208	216	218
F	5	5	5	5	5	7	7	7	7	7	9	9	9	9
G	7	8	8	9	9	9	9	10	10	10	10	11	11	11
H	6	6	8	6	8	6	8	6	8	8	10	6	8	10
I	232	244	258	256	270	268	276	274	286	288	306	296	312	322

One-Row Buttonhole

On the last 7 sts: k1, sl1 purlwise wyif. Then wyib, [sl1, pass slipped st over] x3, return the last slipped st to the passive needle, turn. Take yarn back, then cable cast on 4 sts, bringing the yarn forward before placing the final st onto the passive needle, turn. Sl1 knitwise, then pass the last cast-on st over it. Work to end.

UNDERARM TO EMPIRE LINE

Remove the sleeve sts and commence side decreases as follows:

Row 1 (RS): k7, [p to marker, rm, place sleeve sts on waste yarn, using a provisional method cast on _____(J) sts immediately next to the last st worked, rm] x2, p to last 7 sts, k7.

You should now have _____(K) sts on the needle(s).

Row 2 (WS): [k to centre point of the provisional underarm sts, pm] x2, k to end.

Now alternate the following 2 rows for a total of 4 rows:

RS rows: k7, [p to marker, sm] x2, p to last 7 sts, k7.

WS rows: [k to marker, sm] x2, k to end.

Decrease as follows in the next row, and then in every 4th row until you have worked the decrease row 3 times in total:

Decrease Row (RS): k7, [p to 2 sts before marker, p2tog, sm, ssp] x2, k to end.

When all the decrease rounds have been completed you should have _____(L) sts on the needle(s).

Work a further 2 rows, ending with a RS row. Then, work an applied icord from the WS as follows:

Cast on 3 sts next to the first st on the WS row (ie the last st worked), then *k2, skp, return 3 sts to the passive needle; rep from * until all the bodice sts have been worked. Cast off (bind off) the 3 icord sts, leaving the final st from the cast-off on the needle.

SKIRT

With RS facing pick up and *knit* 7 sts from the edge of the icord that is nearest to the WS, passing the st from the cast-off over the first new st. Then pick up and *purl* all along the same edge of the icord to the last 7 sts. Pick up and *knit* these 7 sts.

You should now have _____(L) sts on your needle.

Set-up row (WS): k_____(M), **pm, [p1 tbl, k2] x5, p1 tbl, pm, k_____(N)**; repeat from ** to ** once, pm, [p1 tbl, k2] x5, p1 tbl, pm, k to end.

RS Rows: k7, [p to marker, sm, work across chart for 'Main Cable Panel', sm] x3, p to last 7 sts, k7.

WS Rows: [k to marker, sm, work across chart for 'Main Cable Panel', sm] x3, k to end.

Alternate these 2 rows until you have worked 3 full repeats of the Main Cable Panel pattern, increasing in the 3rd row and every following 8 rows as follows:

Increase Row (RS): work an m1bp 1 st before the 1st, 3rd and 5th markers, and work an m1fp 1 st after the 2nd, 4th and 6th markers.

Size	32"	34"	36"	38"	40"	42"	44"	46"	48"	50"	52"	54"	56"	58"
J	6	6	6	10	10	14	16	20	22	26	24	30	30	32
K	160	168	178	184	194	200	208	214	226	236	242	248	260	270
L	148	156	166	172	182	188	196	202	214	224	230	236	248	258
M	11	12	14	14	16	16	17	18	20	21	22	22	24	25
N	39	42	45	48	51	54	57	59	63	67	69	72	76	80

After finishing the 3 cable panel repeats you should have ____(O) sts on your needle(s).

Now work as follows, without any further increasing outside the markers:

RS Rows: k7, [p to marker, sm, work across chart for 'Panel A', sm] x3, p to last 7 sts, k7.

WS Rows: [k to marker, sm, work across chart for 'Panel A', sm] x3, k to end.

When you have completed Panel A, continue as follows:

RS Rows: k7, [p to marker, sm, work next 7 sts in pattern as established, work across chart for 'Panel B', work next 7 sts in pattern as established, sm] x3, p to last 7 sts, k7.

WS Rows: [k to marker, sm, work next 7 sts in pattern as established, work across chart for 'Panel B', work next 7 sts in pattern as established, sm] x3, k to end.

After you have worked the row that includes Line 44 of the Panel B chart, commence a garter stitch bottom border as follows:

RS and WS Rows: [k to marker, sm, work next 7 sts in pattern as established, work across chart for 'Panel B', work next 7 sts in pattern as established, sm] x3, k to end.

From the row including line 54 of the Panel B chart, knit 2 sts together at the end of each row. Then, after completing the row that includes line 57 of the Panel B chart, cast off.

SLEEVES (both alike)

Place the sleevecap and provisional underarm sts onto your needle. Then, working from the RS, p1 st, plus the ____(J) provisional underarm sts. Then p____(P) sleevecap sts, pm, work across chart for 'Main Cable Panel'[!] maintaining place in pattern as established, pm, p to end.

You should now have ____(Q) sts on your needle(s).

Join for working in rounds, then work as follows:

Sleeve Rounds: p to marker, sm, work across chart for 'Main Cable Panel'[!], sm, p to end.

When you have completed approximately 38 rounds, ending after a line 2, 14 or 16 of the 'Main Cable Panel' chart, switch to working Panel A[!] between the markers.

After you have worked the round that includes Line 47 of the Panel A chart, alternate the following 2 rounds for the final 6 rounds:

Round 1: p to marker, sm, work across chart for 'Panel A'[!], sm, k to end.

Round 2: k to marker, sm, work across chart for 'Panel A'[!], sm, p to end.

After the final round, p to the first panel marker, then cast off.

[!]When knitting in the round, follow all chart lines from right to left.

Size	32"	34"	36"	38"	40"	42"	44"	46"	48"	50"	52"	54"	56"	58"
O	184	192	202	208	218	224	232	238	250	260	266	272	284	294
P	16	17	18	18	19	20	21	21	22	22	25	24	25	26
Q	55	57	59	63	65	71	75	79	83	87	91	95	97	101

Panel A

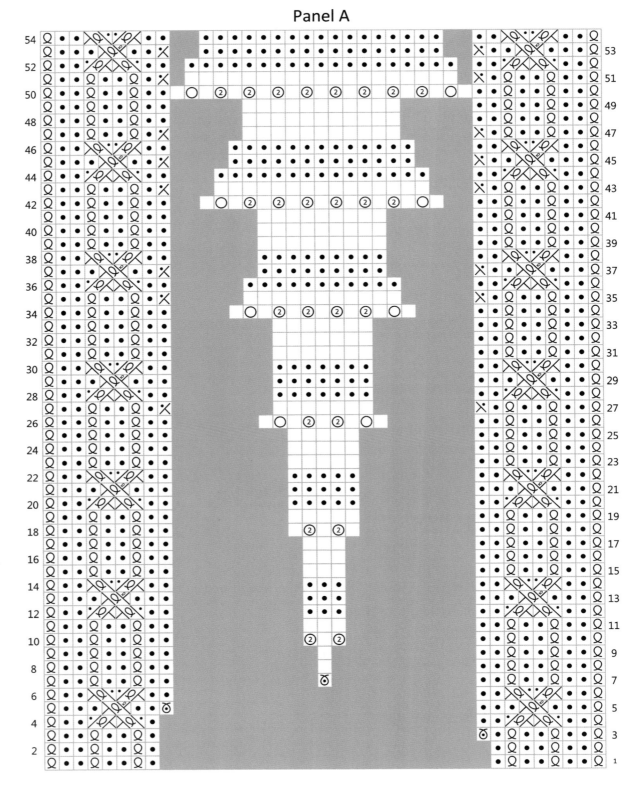

In the row after making double yarnovers ('yo twice'), knit the 1st yarn over and drop the 2nd.

Panel B

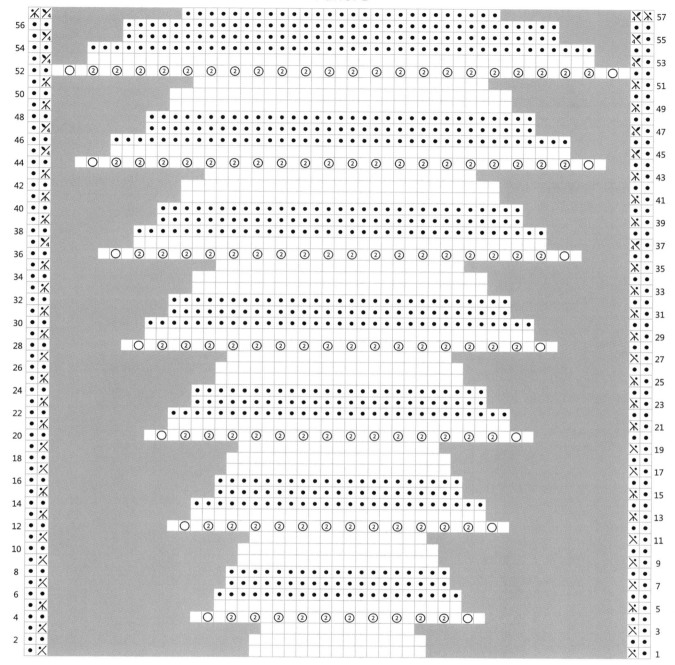

In the row after making double yarnovers ('yo twice'), knit the 1st yarn over and drop the 2nd.

HOOD

Working with the RS facing you at the neckline, pick up and *knit* 7 sts from the edge of the icord that is nearest to the WS, passing the st from the cast-off over the first new st. Then pick up and *purl* all along the same edge of the icord to the last 7 sts. Pick up and *knit* these 7 sts.

You should now have _____(A) sts on your needle.

Set-up Row (WS): k7, **pm, [p1 tbl, k2] x3, p1 tbl, pm**, k to last 17 sts, repeat from ** to **, k to end.

Now alternate the following 2 rows until you have worked 59 pattern rows in total, ending with a RS row.

RS Hood Rows: k to marker, **sm, work across chart for 'Hood Cable Panel', sm**, p to marker, repeat from ** to **, k to end.

WS Hood Rows: [k to marker, sm, work across chart for 'Hood Cable Panel', sm] x2, k to end.

Set up for the hood decreases as follows:

Set-up Row (WS): k7, **sm, work across chart for 'Hood Cable Panel', sm**, k_____(R), pm, k22, pm, k to marker, repeat from ** to **, k to end.

Continuing hood pattern as established, decrease as follows in the next and every following RS row until you have worked 10 decrease rows in total, ending with a RS decrease row:

Decrease Rows (RS): p2tog immediately after the 3rd marker, ssp immediately before the 4th marker.

Final row (WS): work in pattern as established to the 3rd marker, rm, k1. Then, with the right sides facing each other, graft the two halves of the row together using kitchener stitch. It is possible to graft in pattern if you wish. A tutorial for grafting in pattern may be found at the 'Knitting Daily' website.

FINISHING

Weave in all ends then block to the dimensions shown on the next page.

HOOD CABLE PANEL

Size	32"	34"	36"	38"	40"	42"	44"	46"	48"	50"	52"	54"	56"	58"
R	8	12	15	16	19	20	20	21	23	24	27	28	32	33

BLOCKING DIAGRAM

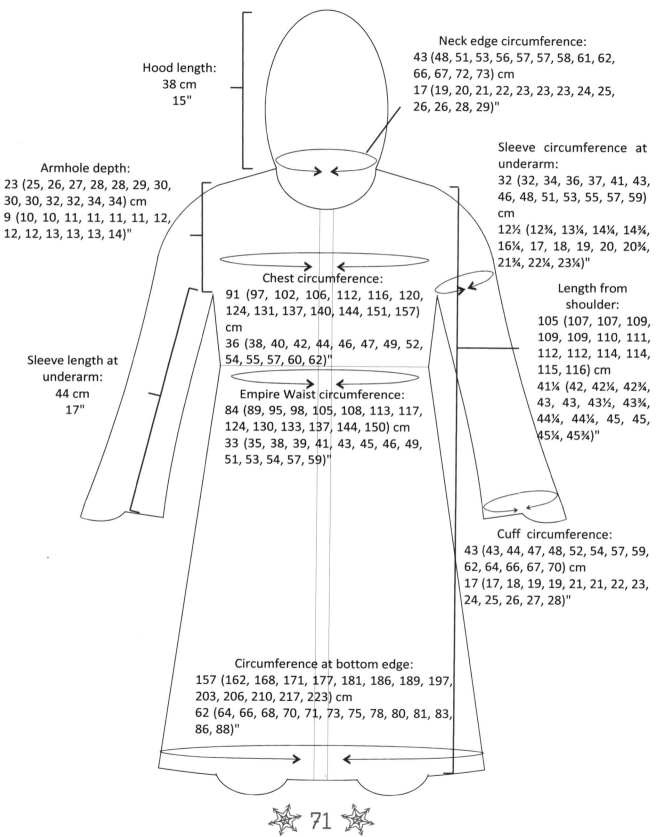

Hood length:
38 cm
15"

Neck edge circumference:
43 (48, 51, 53, 56, 57, 57, 58, 61, 62,
66, 67, 72, 73) cm
17 (19, 20, 21, 22, 23, 23, 23, 24, 25,
26, 26, 28, 29)"

Armhole depth:
23 (25, 26, 27, 28, 28, 29, 30,
30, 30, 32, 32, 34, 34) cm
9 (10, 10, 11, 11, 11, 11, 12,
12, 12, 13, 13, 13, 14)"

Sleeve circumference at
underarm:
32 (32, 34, 36, 37, 41, 43,
46, 48, 51, 53, 55, 57, 59)
cm
12½ (12¾, 13¼, 14¼, 14¾,
16¼, 17, 18, 19, 20, 20¾,
21¾, 22¼, 23¼)"

Chest circumference:
91 (97, 102, 106, 112, 116, 120,
124, 131, 137, 140, 144, 151, 157)
cm
36 (38, 40, 42, 44, 46, 47, 49, 52,
54, 55, 57, 60, 62)"

Length from
shoulder:
105 (107, 107, 109,
109, 109, 110, 111,
112, 112, 114, 114,
115, 116) cm
41¼ (42, 42¼, 42¾,
43, 43, 43½, 43¾,
44¼, 44¼, 45, 45,
45¼, 45¾)"

Sleeve length at
underarm:
44 cm
17"

Empire Waist circumference:
84 (89, 95, 98, 105, 108, 113, 117,
124, 130, 133, 137, 144, 150) cm
33 (35, 38, 39, 41, 43, 45, 46, 49,
51, 53, 54, 57, 59)"

Cuff circumference:
43 (43, 44, 47, 48, 52, 54, 57, 59,
62, 64, 66, 67, 70) cm
17 (17, 18, 19, 19, 21, 21, 22, 23,
24, 25, 26, 27, 28)"

Circumference at bottom edge:
157 (162, 168, 171, 177, 181, 186, 189, 197,
203, 206, 210, 217, 223) cm
62 (64, 66, 68, 70, 71, 73, 75, 78, 80, 81, 83,
86, 88)"

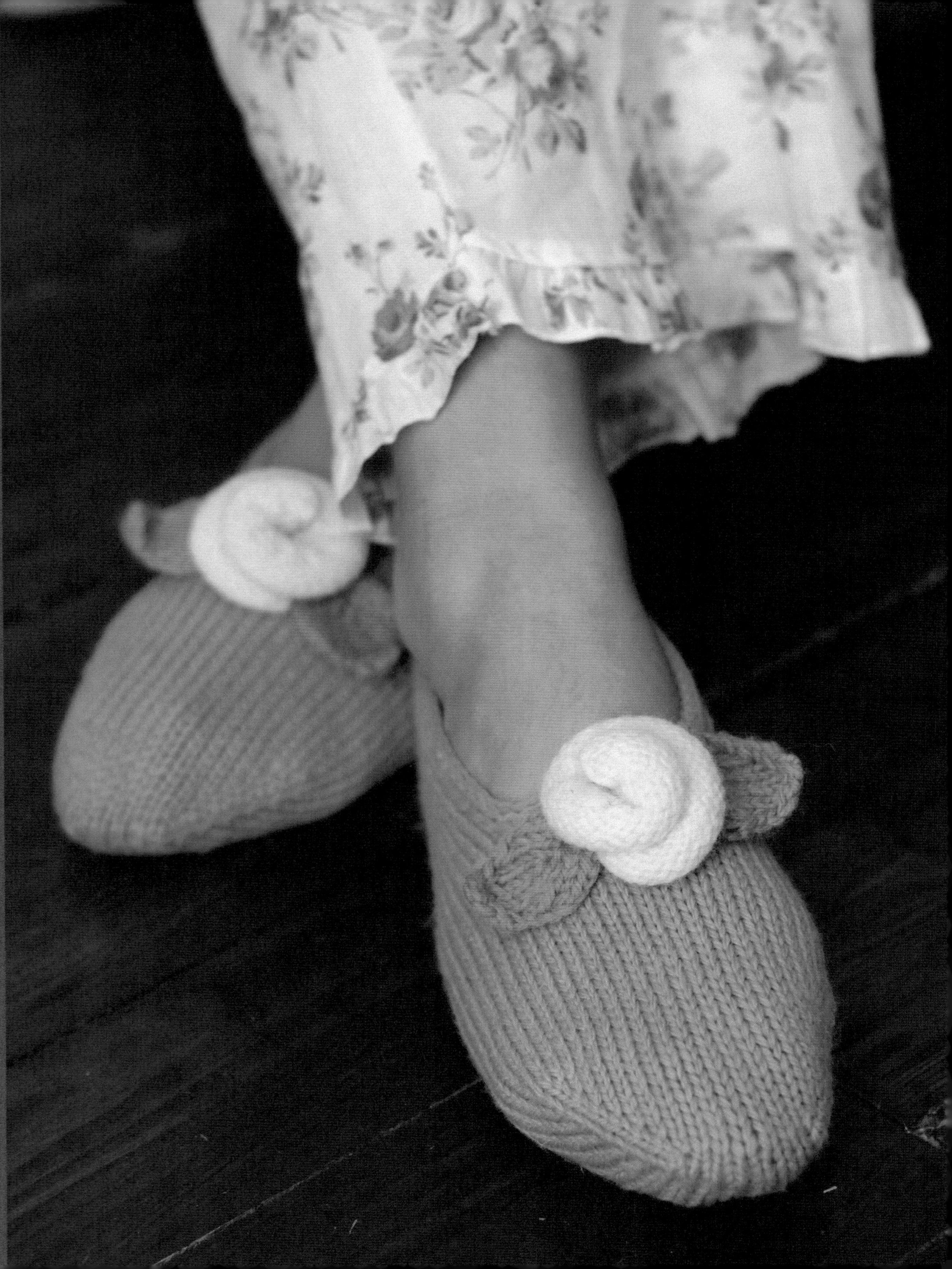

SIZE

To fit 20½(23:25½)cm/8(9:10)" foot circumference. Foot length is customized.

MATERIALS

Feltable worsted-weight wool yarn in three colours. Approximately 60–80g of main colour (120–160 metres / 132–176 yards) of main colour, and 10g each (20 metres / 22 yards) of leaf colour and your chosen rose colour.

The pictured slippers were made with 'Cascade 220' in 'Robin Egg Blue', 'White', and 'Lime Heather'.

NEEDLES AND NOTIONS

4mm/US 6 needles (or size required to achieve the specified tension) for your preferred method of small diameter circular knitting, and 3.75mm/US 5 needles.

2 stitchmarkers. Darning/yarn needle.

TENSION/GAUGE

22 sts and 32 rounds per 10cm/4" in stocking stitch/stockinette knitted in the round on the larger needle(s).

A specific gauge for the leaves and roses is not required. Use the smaller needle(s), then felt them to an appropriate size.

Instructions

ROSES *(make 1 for each slipper)*

With your chosen rose colour and the smaller needle(s), cast on 45 sts. Work 7 rows of st-st, beginning and ending with a purl row. Then decrease as follows:

Rows 8: s2kp x 15. *(15 sts)*

Rows 9 & 11: purl.

Row 10: s2kp x 5. *(5 sts)*

Row 12: s4kp. *(1 st)*

Leaving a short tail for weaving in, break the yarn and pull it through the last st. Weave in all ends, then twist into the rose shape.

LEAVES *(make 2 for each slipper)*

With the smaller needle and your leaf coloured yarn, cast on 3 sts.

Row 1: k1, m3, k1. *(5 sts)*

Row 2 and all even-numbered rows: purl.

Rows 3 & 5: k to centre st, m3, k to end. *(7, 9 sts)*

Rows 7, 9, and 11: skp, k to last 2 sts, k2tog. *(7, 5, 3 sts)*

Row 13: sk2p. *(1 st)*

Leaving a short tail for weaving in, break the yarn and pull it through the last st.

Felt the roses and the leaves according to your preferred method. The roses in the sample were felted in a front-loader washing machine with eco washing balls.

Meanwhile, knit the slippers, following the instructions on the next page twice to make a pair.

TOE

With MC and the larger needle(s) cast on 12(16:18) sts using either the 'Turkish' method or 'Judy's magic cast-on'. You should have 6(8:9) sts on each of two needles.

Working in rounds continue as follows:

Round 1: [k6(8:9), pm] x2.

Round 2: k1, lia, k to 1 st before marker, lib, k1, sm, k to 1 st before marker, lib, k1, sm.

Round 3: k to marker, sm, k1, lia, k to marker, sm.

Repeat Rounds 2 and 3 until you have increased the total st count to 40(44:50) sts

Continue in st-st without any further increasing until the toe measures 10cm/4" from the cast-on. Remove the markers in the final round.

FOOT OPENING

Row 1: k5(5:6), place the next 10(12:13) sts onto waste yarn, turn.

Row 2: p30(32:37), turn.

Continue working in st-st rows until the slipper measures 2½cm/1" less than the total desired foot length, ending with a purl row.

HEEL TURN

Row 1: k19(21:24), turn.

Row 2: sl1 purlwise, p7(9:10), turn.

Row 3: sl1 purlwise, k6(8:9), skp, turn.

Row 4: sl1 purlwise, p6(8:9), p2tog, turn.

Repeat Rows 3 & 4 until all the side sts have been decreased away, leaving just the 8(10:11) heel sts.

ICORD EDGING

Cable cast on 3 sts immediately next to the last st worked. Then, with RS facing, work an applied icord edging on the heel sts as follows: *k2, skp, return 3 sts to the passive needle; rep from * until all the heel sts have been worked.

Continue working applied icord around the foot opening, picking up 1 st for every 2 rows at the slipper edge as follows: *k2, sl1 knitwise, pick up and knit 1 st from the edge of the slipper, psso, return 3 sts to the passive needle; rep from * until you reach the removed toe sts.

To close any holes at the corner before the removed sts, pick up 1 or 2 extra sts there and apply icord to them as previously instructed .

Place the removed toe sts onto a needle with the 3 icord sts before them, then apply icord to these as for the heel. Apply icord to the second side of the slipper as you did to the first.

On reaching the heel break off the yarn, leaving a 20cm/8" tail for grafting. Graft the 3 icord sts to the cast-on sts at the start of the icord.

FINISHING

Weave in all ends on the inside of each slipper. When the roses and leaves have dried, carefully position them on the slipper toes and sew them in place using your leaf-coloured yarn.

Abbreviations

bdtc = RS: place next st on cable needle and hold in back, knit next st tbl, knit st from cable needle tbl.
WS: as RS but purl both sts tbl.

btc = RS: place next st on cable needle and hold in back, knit next st tbl, purl st from cable needle.
WS: as RS but knit 1st st as normal (not tbl), then purl st from cable needle tbl.

CC = contrast colour

cdd = sl2 together knitwise, k1, psso.

eor = end of row/round

fdtc = RS: place next st on cable needle and hold in front, knit next st tbl, knit st from cable needle tbl.
WS: as RS but purl both sts tbl.

ftc = RS: place next st on cable needle and hold in front, purl next st, knit st from cable needle tbl.
WS: as RS but purl 1st st tbl, then knit st from cable needle as normal (not tbl).

k = knit

k1b = knit 1 st tbl.

k2tog = knit 2 sts together.

k3tog = knit 3 sts together.

k4tog = knit 4 sts together.

lia = lifted increase after: insert the passive needle under the nearest side of the st 2 rows below the last st made. Knit into the back of the st from this position.

lib = lifted increase before: insert the working needle under the nearest side of the st below the next st to be worked. Lift the the st onto the passive needle and knit it.

m1b = from the back lift the strand between sts onto the passive needle and knit it.

m1bp = from the back lift the strand between sts onto the passive needle and purl it.

m1f = from the front lift the strand between sts onto the passive needle and knit it tbl.

m1fp = from the front lift the strand between sts onto the passive needle and purl it tbl.

m3 = k1, p1, k1, all into the same st.

MC = main colour

p = purl

p2tog = purl 2 sts together.

p3tog = purl 3 sts together.

p4tog = purl 4 sts together.

pb = place bead: wyif sl1 purlwise, pull up a bead, then take yarn back.

pm = place marker

psso = pass slipped st(s) over.

rep = repeat

rm = remove marker

RS = right side

s2kp = 1 at a time sl2 knitwise, k1, psso.

s3kp = 1 at a time sl3 knitwise, k1, psso.

s3p = 1 at a time sl3 knitwise, return slipped sts to passive needle then p3tog tbl.

s4kp = 1 at a time sl4 knitwise, k1, psso.

s4p = 1 at a time, sl4 knitwise, return slipped sts to passive needle then p4tog tbl.

sk2p = sl1 knitwise, k2tog, psso.

skp = sl1 knitwise, k1, psso.

sl = slip st(s) either knitwise or purlwise as instructed.

sm = slip marker

ssp = 1 at a time sl2 knitwise, return to passive needle then p2tog tbl.

st(s) = stitch(es)

st-st = stocking stitch (stockinette)

tbl = through the back loop(s)

WS = wrong side

wyib = with the yarn at the back

wyif = with the yarn in front

yo = yarn over

Chart Symbols

☐ RS: knit WS: purl	⋀ sk2p
• RS: purl WS: knit	⋀ cdd
▨ no stitch	Ⴘ lia
○ yo	Ⴒ lib
② yo twice	Ω RS: k1b WS: p tbl
⋋ k2tog	◆ CC
⋌ skp	◉ m1fp
⋏ k3tog	⑪ pb
⋌ s2kp	btc
⋰₄ k4tog	ftc
₄⋱ s3kp	bdtc
✕ p2tog	fdtc
✕ ssp	
✕ p3tog	
✕ s3p	
⋎₄ p4tog	
₄✕ s4p	

Thanks

Many people were involved in the making of this book. I especially thank the following:

- Karen Butler, my technical editor, whose exhaustive examination of the knitting instructions and general text has made a vast difference to the book's quality.

- Verity Britton, fab photographer and cover designer, and her husband Chris, photo editor and layout assistant.

- Georgiana Mannion and Ruby Chohan, our beautiful models.

- Marie Wright, my beloved twin-sister, who knitted samples for the Truly, Prom, Summer Seas and Sweetheart Mitts patterns, and who constantly gives me highly valued general support.

- Heidi Beckmann, who knitted the sample for the Indian Summer pattern. Her knitting is so incredibly neat that many people have asked if the sample was knitted on a machine!

- David Kingstone, the most patient and supportive husband that anybody could wish for. I am very happy that he is mine!

- Daniel, Tom and Toby, my wonderful boys, who have patiently waited for many late meals as I worked on this book, and who constantly express pride and interest in what I do.

- Margaret Leach, my mother, who first taught me to knit. I love you Mum!

Support

For support with any of the knitting techniques used in this book, please visit www.annkingstone.com. The 'Knitting School' there includes a variety of my own tutorials, including online video tutorials. The 'Support' area of the site also includes a page with links to various other online tutorials.

5762582R00045

Printed in Great Britain
by Amazon.co.uk, Ltd.,
Marston Gate.